Lessons with Kiarostami

Lessons with Kiarostami

Edited by Paul Cronin
Foreword by Mike Leigh

Sticking Place Books
New York

© Sticking Place Books 2015

www.stickingplacebooks.com
www.lessonswithkiarostami.com
www.filmmakertrilogy.com

Design by Ryan Bojanovic

ISBN 978-1-942782-47-6

For Gabrielle

Foreword
by Mike Leigh

Every independent filmmaker likes to think that he or she is unique, and many of us possibly are, a bit. But nobody is more unique than my good friend Abbas Kiarostami.

Here he is, one of the greatest of us all, the originator and master of the minimalist epic, the visionary who has raised the cinema of humanity to an unprecedented level of purity, the reluctant teacher who modestly confronts us with truths so profound that they blind with their luminous clairvoyance, the outrageous provocateur with an exhilarating capacity to make statements about his ideas and methods which will so shock that you will likely howl out loud, albeit joyfully.

Nuggets of Abbas' wisdom and hard-won insights are scattered throughout this inspiring book like plums in a pudding. Personal, practical, professional, humorous, emotional, philosophical, artistic and technical, they are all profoundly useful to the aspiring filmmaker. But while Abbas gently guides us, ultimately he leaves it up to each of us to find the way to our own truth. As such, this book is sure to become a cornerstone of film literature.

Over the past two decades, Abbas Kiarostami – the Iranian film director of *Where is the Friend's House?*, *Life and Nothing More*, *Through the Olive Trees*, *Close-Up*, *Taste of Cherry*, *The Wind Will Carry Us*, *Ten*, *Shirin*, *Certified Copy* and *Like Someone in Love* – has appeared regularly at festivals and on campuses, where he has worked closely for several days with young filmmakers, shepherding them and their projects, sending them out with cameras, then screening and discussing the results. This book has been pieced together from notes made over ten years at a number of workshops (London, Marrakech, Potenza, Oslo, New York, Syracuse) and placed alongside material accumulated during numerous conversations with Kiarostami, some at his home in Tehran, some recorded during workshop interludes.

Kiarostami has long been aware that, as students, we glean as much from each other as from our instructors, that producing a stream of work is the most efficient approach to learning, that the best way to understand the intricacies of filmmaking is to inhabit an environment within which a group of eager, creative, receptive and disciplined people can strive communally. At their best, his workshops are just these settings, physical spaces where ideas are developed and short films made at speed. Direct lecturing is sidestepped. Instead, troops (ideally with some level of experience) are assembled, diversity of opinion and inclusiveness nurtured, a succession of leaps into the unknown taken. As it does in these live sessions, dialogue between teacher and students in this book comes relatively early because it is during the first days of such interactions that the ideas flow thickest and fastest. Once a certain tone is set, a pace is achieved, students are sent outside to film, to make good on their workshopped ideas, and the results are eventually unveiled. Critique sessions and deliberation follow, throughout which Kiarostami – describing, through an interpreter, how he might have done it – assists us in cleaning our metaphorical glasses and embarking upon future work with fresh vision.

No doubt it has all been done before, by someone with a similar level of expertise, by a filmmaker as adept and charismatic. I would never insist upon the singularity of Kiarostami's workshops, neither the ideas he puts forth nor his method of explanation. But the straightforward is always new and bracing to someone, worthy of articulation both on the page and in the classroom (how to argue with the fervour of some students?), so it's difficult not to delight in Kiarostami's approach. Beyond this, there is much to admire: his vision, forswearing of dogma, warm-heartedness and self-sufficiency, quietude, mythic quality – the wanderer, the man in the desert – and lack of caprice. All these qualities suit me down to the ground and have helped reconnect me to some of the intangibles in life, to things boundless. And who doesn't envy Kiarostami's involvement in his own inventiveness, an engagement so profound that – benignly closed off, by temperament and terrain, yet so very productive – he is scarcely touched by the work of other artists and filmmakers, theorists and critics? This is a man who can do nothing but his own thing, who could turn his back and be satisfied with spending the rest of his days alone, processing the contents of his mind.

Also enthralling are his sensibilities as an artist and skills as a filmmaker. Adept at sleight of hand, the apparent simplicity of Kiarostami's films is deceptive, belying the complexity of their arrangement, precision and intricate design. The audacious conceptual and technical achievements behind his work are almost never immediately apparent, which means the films can appear uncontrolled and casual, at times even amateurish. Another viewing of his near-invisible process, a closer look at his cinema – in which the pendulum swings gently back and forth from fiction to non-fiction – in tandem with remarks made in this book, may yield a different assessment. I commend anyone who is able to teach us all we need to know about the crucial notion of suspense by presenting little more than the image of waves crashing against rocks, upon which lie, unprotected, three eggs. Throughout Kiarostami's seventeen-minute film *Seagull Eggs*, we know what will likely happen next, but just when and precisely how is up for grabs. Kiarostami's is, among other achievements, a dynamic cinema of evocation, motivated by a creative spirit that can be summed by Albert Camus, who in 1938 wrote that "La véritable œuvre d'art est celle qui dit moins."

We initiates and acolytes who have attended his pedagogic assemblies, who are lucky to have travelled with Kiarostami and basked in his glow, respond as Marlene Dietrich did after time spent with Orson Welles: "When I talk with him," she effused, "I feel like a plant that has been watered." Just when you think there is nothing more of interest to say on the subject at hand, Kiarostami will say something interesting, approaching an idea from a different angle, returning to it days after it was first expounded upon, at all times reinforcing key concepts. He is a seemingly endless fount, and during the workshops I attended consistently directed his thoughts with nuance of timing and tone. Moreover, of the participants I befriended, it was evident that several were being pushed against a wall, for a rare moment required to decipher everything for themselves. They were suddenly and startlingly confronted by the need to make certain definitive decisions, to answer questions they might otherwise never have considered or even avoided for their difficulty. By responding to such an occasion, these students – nourished by the lessons of Kiarostami – became steadily emboldened, full of lively desires and ambitions, with a new degree of self-realisation, self-enquiry, self-awareness. I found it exciting to watch, and expect everyone else did, too, including Kiarostami, who revels in the successes and hard work of others. As the fourteenth-century Persian poet Hafez tells us, always carry fire in your heart and ensure that tears are welling. Anything less is indifference.

What follows is not a traditional interview book or manual of filmmaking, still less a survey of Iranian cinema or study of Kiarostami's films. Instead, the text is a distillation of techniques and working methods, an attempt to capture the essence of an often mysterious experience. It is a construct, an interpretation and careful condensation of filtered fragments that comprise something of a methodology, written in the first person, from Kiarostami's point of view. It reflects a subjective appreciation of his artful approach to storytelling, of his philosophy of life and feelings about the world around him, and recounts his perspicacity and orientation towards clarity. It is a poetics, a treatise on the creation and meaning of cinema that expresses aspects of Kiarostami's aesthetic sensibility. It is, most importantly, a series of practical guideposts structured around broad principles.

In a recent interview, Mike Leigh spoke of his belief that "you cannot really film or show the creative moment on the screen... You can evoke it, you can imply it, you can present the justification of images, but the actual creation itself is elusive and I would say, in strict terms, unfilmable." Such things are, presumably, equally untranslatable into words. But this book is nonetheless an attempt to convey on the page the thoughts and impulses behind Kiarostami's creative moments as a filmmaker, photographer and poet. Perhaps, hopefully, a touch enigmatic, it asks of its readers what Kiarostami – endearingly, admirably, in a mode of eternal aspiration and discovery – asks of those who watch his cinema: that they unpack it all themselves, in their own time. Like his films, *Lessons with Kiarostami* poses more questions than it answers. It would never presume to be the final word.

Images of Kiarostami, workshop chief, linger in mind. Taking photographs through the windows of a car speeding along rainy roads of Southern Italy. Sharing red wine at every dinner. Strolling, camera in hand, up into the mountains near Marrakech. Standing, stone-faced, on a backstreet, one bitterly cold Manhattan morning, as a crew filmed its short. Four remembrances particularly endure, each summing up qualities that intrigue and impress: his visual and auditory acuity, his craftsmanship, his apparent serenity, his ability to find majesty in places few others would think to look. At one point during our time together in a spacious room in South Kensington, during the 2005 London workshop, as sunshine streamed through the windows, he alerted me to a fantastical design on the carpet and noted, "What an extraordinary shadow!" One afternoon during the Marrakech workshop later that year, he wanted to show his film *Five* to Martin Scorsese, who had stopped by as a guest lecturer. A room was found and someone placed black paper across the window to block the light. Kiarostami wasn't happy with the result, so it was taken down and he undertook the job himself, first by studying the shape of the window from several feet away, then cutting and folding some wrapping paper. When finally he placed it over the glass, the piece fit perfectly. At another workshop, in upstate New York, the seventy-five-year-old Kiarostami spoke of his three months in Prague more than four decades earlier. He recited for me the announcement made by the city trams' loudspeaker system, something he had listened to for weeks but never since, and even today doesn't know the meaning of. In Tehran, I spent an evening at an artist's studio, watching Kiarostami stare into a large industrial printer which, millimetre by millimetre, was gently sending out into the world one of his photographs. Hours later it was still only halfway done. The monastic Kiarostami sat, watching intently, in silence, as the image steadily rolled onto the floor. The attention to process was, for him, a form of meditation.

Whence *Lessons with Kiarostami*? From fascination with his films, photographs and poetry (which one day may well be included in the canon of modern Persian verse). From interest in

Kiarostami's idea of "re-educating the viewer's gaze." From years of attachment to his workshops and a corresponding excitement and wondrous bemusement. From a perhaps conceited belief in a responsibility to document these challenging and fleeting sessions. From enthusiasm felt while reading the work of a handful of Kiarostami's most passionate and perceptive exponents. From dissatisfaction with Kiarostami's own *10 on Ten*, in which for ninety minutes he exercises a didactic urge by discussing filmmaking methods. Having spent so much time with him, I felt there was a more effective way of representing those ideas, which pivot around his desire – also the hope of this book – to be of use to the average film student.

Three final thoughts. First, any reader who admires Kiarostami's films, and wishes to think further on his approach to making them, might be interested in the pages that follow. But one needn't be particularly familiar with Kiarostami's work to appreciate this book. Indeed, to press further in that direction, one might take little or no notice of the world of cinema, yet still find something of significance. Second, the restless and energetic Kiarostami continues to make films, to roam, to lend his efforts to workshops around the world, which means that while this book is offered to readers in a finished form, it is a project still in progress. Third, an immersion in Kiarostami's world involves investigation not just of his films, but also his epodic photography and imagistic poetry, a process that reveals compelling correspondences between all three, as well as exposing the fountainhead of the cinema he is known for around the world: Persian poetry, ancient and modern. This is one reason why the publication of *Lessons with Kiarostami* is accompanied by what can be looked upon as a massive appendix: a collection of translations of Kiarostami's original verse and his selections from a range of Persian poets, including Nima, Hafez, Saadi and Rumi.

This book is part of an unplanned trilogy that explores the working methods and pedagogic philosophy of three filmmakers (Werner Herzog and Alexander Mackendrick are the other two), all somehow linked by a search for what Herzog calls "adequate imagery." Kiarostami, always in search of the unfamilar, was never too excited about what I was planning, though did carefully scrutinise the Persian version of this book, at which point I believe he came to see its value and utility, and emphatically lent it – and our poetry project – his imprimatur.

Support and assistance for this project has come from the British Academy. Photography by the inscrutable Presley Parks. If my experiences at the workshops were the meat and potatoes of this book, my trip to Iran and time with Kiarostami in his home environment added much needed seasoning to hundreds of pages of handwritten notes. Special gratitude to Negin Fazeli – trusted consigliere in Tehran – who provided such a captivating introduction to Persian culture and society. While translating this book into Persian (published alongside the English edition), the enlightened Sohrab Mahdavi offered a vital commentary on its themes. His contributions and knowledge of the Sufi lexicon underpin my entire Kiarostami project. The erudite Iman Tavassoly opened up the incandescent world of Persian poetry to me, for which I give deep and humble thanks. Working with Iman as co-translator has immeasurably improved *Lessons with Kiarostami*. And thanks to Abbas, a hearty guide on the path, who lays out here a model of what a coherent and convincing film school might be, who on the journey always carries a most powerful lantern. Eloquent is the achievement of a wisdom that never strives to be lasting.

The Editor

There's land untaken next to mine. Each of you can have a hundred and sixty acres, and then we'll have six hundred and forty acres all in one piece. The grass is deep and rich, and the soil wants only turning. No rocks, Thomas, to make your plough turn somersaults, no ledges sticking out. We'll make a new community here if you'll come.

John Steinbeck, *To a God Unknown*

قطع این مرحله بی همرهی خضر مکن
ظلمات است بترس از خطر گمراهی

Do not undertake the journey on this road
without the company of Khidr, the guide of souls.
Beware of losing yourself in the darkness.

Hafez

As a playwright I should consider I had done my duty if I succeeded in a play of mine in putting a question in such a way that from then on the members of the audience were unable to live without an answer. But it must be their answer, their own, which they can provide only in the framework of their own lives.

Max Frisch, *Sketchbook 1946 – 1949*

I've sailored. I've been there and back. I'm here where I'm needed.

Harold Pinter, *No Man's Land*

Those who are clever in imagination are far more pleased with themselves than prudent men could reasonably be.

Pascal, *Pensées*

I have nothing to teach you. In fact, I never refer to what I do at meetings like these as teaching, because I don't like the word. Some people who find themselves talking to groups of young filmmakers insist there are specific "rules" that should be obeyed. But cinema isn't anchored to any particular methodology or set of ideas. Filmmaking can't be taught the way so many other things can, which means that what I will be saying this week shouldn't be taken as gospel. Although I am of a certain age – older than you all – I have never been one to offer advice and tell people how they should do their work. My job is merely to make suggestions and talk about my own particular way of doing things, which is one method among many, and which to this day continues to evolve.

I have done a handful of these workshops before, and have learned something at every one of them. Days like these are full of clarifying experiences for me because I can take a step back and think like a beginner. Whenever I make a feature film, I am under the shadow and in the clutches of a producer. It isn't easy to try new things within the expensive structures of professional film production, which brings with it certain responsibilities and therefore closes off opportunities for experimentation, even though that desire remains steadfast within. But here, with you, I have the chance to re-encounter my youthful and naïve feelings about cinema. I find myself thinking about my own films as I listen to participants – I am reluctant to call you students – and watch your work. And, of course, I am not immune to instruction myself. Based on time spent with filmmakers in Turin a few years ago, I went home to Tehran and changed the ending of the film I was making.

My job here is no more important than what each of you can individually bring to the group. We aren't here to judge one another or impose our tastes. The objective is to help unleash your motivations so you can make films we can look at together. My hope is that this will be a conversation, a dialogue. We are all links in the chain, ideally full of ideas about each other's work, hopefully flowing with empathy for one another. Exercising our competitive spirit isn't what this is about.

1

During the first days of previous workshops, I have found myself yearning to walk into a room like this and discover it empty, with everyone outside busy filming. The most frustrating thing at events like these is being unable to persuade participants to get to work. It's discouraging to hear people tell me that what I am asking them to do is difficult. It's like being kicked in the shins. The heavier the burden, the more inertia there is. Fear of failure can be paralysing, which is why the least experienced participants are often those with the fewest concerns and the most powerful forward momentum. They seem to find it easier to get out there and do the work. Perhaps we should emulate them this week, with the experienced taking their cues from the newcomers. At the last workshop there were more than one thousand applicants for thirty places, and several people who hadn't been accepted showed up anyway, standing and listening at the door, so the organisers decided to allow them in. Those unofficial participants were the first to ask questions. They were the first to go out and make films and bring them back to show everyone. One woman made a short we all enjoyed. Someone asked her what her background was. "I work in the sandwich shop across the road," she explained. The seasoned filmmakers stayed in their seats while this young sandwich-maker dashed out to make a film.

The focus of our time here shouldn't be on making films into which you can pack every trick you have ever learned. I am not looking for fully realised ideas, much less masterpieces, the sort of things that require meticulous planning and can be added to your résumé. There is no such thing as a perfect film, only a film with fewer errors than the one before it. Coming up with an idea and starting production is what's most important. Find a partner or small cohort to work with, if that will help you awaken faster and more fully. Don't be so proud that you won't ask for help. Accept ideas from anyone. It's often more efficient if everyone pools their individual talents and resources. A hunting party can be more effective than the lone warrior. And be quick. The days will blow past faster than you can imagine. Pace yourself and learn from mistakes. If you aren't happy with what you end up with, it's not worth a minute of worry. Just put it aside and start again. We need films that are like pieces of paper you can crumple and throw away if you aren't content. Small projects keep us agile for bigger ones. A short film might be makeshift, but at least it exists.

Listen to what everyone around you is saying, not just me. Together we can provide solutions to some of your filmmaking problems. Nothing is ever completely beyond repair. Most of the time, however, I suspect that you will be able to answer your own questions. I would never think of shirking my responsibilities, but thanks to the digital cameras available to us, you have every opportunity to explore and discover your creativity in your own time, on your own terms. The days we spend together aren't about me teaching you so much as me encouraging you to search within yourself for what is required.

I never had any formal film training, which has both advantages and disadvantages. When I started out as a filmmaker, I was unaware of how the profession functioned, which means I was unafraid. I simply didn't know what there was to be fearful of. To those already graduated from film school, don't be too proud of having received a formal education in cinema. School has never been the only place to acquire knowledge. Guidance can be useful, but you shouldn't need anyone to tell you to read a book or make a film. You either want to learn or you don't. Too many people spend four years paying for what can be digested and understood in four weeks.

I have always considered the best film school the one you construct yourself, powered by your own needs and motivations. Educate yourself by watching, by training your eye, then by doing, by going out and making films. It isn't difficult to make an uninteresting film, but worthy projects are more complex and often have little to do with the resources of a film school. They are the result of compulsions you are unable to shake off, no matter how hard you might try. They are the product of an unwavering imagination.

I enjoy listening to stories, so hopefully over the coming days I will be doing less and less talking. There are few skills more invigorating than being able to tell a story to an expectant crowd. It could be about anything. The drunken revelry and mischief you were involved in last night, a quiet breakfast this morning, the argument you had with your wife, an incident at work. You might think that occurences like these have no value to you as storytellers, as filmmakers, but together we can find something worthy in what what at first glance seems mundane. Good films emerge from the simplest and smallest moments. Look with fresh eyes at the daily banalities of life and see how fascinating they actually are. As filmmakers, our job is to observe, recall, then represent on screen.

The better you observe, the more intensely you bear witness to the world, the better your work will be. If there are stories that you are bursting with, use this opportunity to tell them to others.

The basis of the films you make over the coming days is probably already in your head: the characters, landscapes and scenarios they contain. My job – the job of everyone here – is to draw these things out. Sometimes a fragment of dialogue or image in my mind can be spun into an entire drama. The starting point of every one of my films is a moment either told to me or that I witnessed, then kept close until I found some creative use for it. My head remains full of stories I haven't yet found time to unpack. Eventually one resonates in distinct and sometimes unfamiliar ways, taking on new importance and perhaps becoming the source of a film.

When I select participants for the school in Tehran where I have worked over the years, I don't ask what they know about cinema or if they have ever made a film. I ask them to tell me a story. What someone comes up with and the skill with which they tell it – knowing when to pause for dramatic effect, how to introduce new characters, what to leave out, when to bring the tale to an end – are the best ways of knowing whether this person might be a competent filmmaker. Understanding the relationship between storyteller and listener is essential. One of Rumi's poems tells us that if there is eloquence, enthusiasm and energy within someone, it is drawn out by the listener of the tale. What pushed me to make *Certified Copy* was the intensity and enthusiasm of Juliette Binoche's response to the story I told her, the reaction in her eyes, the spontaneous movement of her head. I never had any intention of turning that story into a film, and am sure that had I told it to anyone else I would never have made *Certified Copy.* So start telling us your ideas and see how we respond. Our reactions will let you know how compelling they are.

What we discuss and what I say isn't right or wrong. It's like going to a psychiatrist. We are just talking, expressing our ideas to each other. I am not here to push my opinions on you. My opinions are nothing but my films. The most useful thing I can do is make my feelings clear and describe my way of doing things, which ultimately might not work for you. All I ask is that you draw your own conclusions, make your own assessments, and – because there is never one way of accomplishing things – experiment. We are here together, which means the joys and misfortunes you experience this week will be shared by everyone. We are all comrades together, from all over the world, united by a single language. Film binds us together in extraordinary ways and will enable us to have a common experience over the coming days. Engage. Express yourself. Don't sit on the sidelines. Be the first to speak. You and your ideas are the gems. I am merely the metal chain linking everything together.

❦ ❦ ❦

I am often asked at the start of these workshops what sort of films I expect from participants. The most useful response I can give is a description of the sort of cinema I am inclined towards, both to watch and to make. Every story that moves and interests me has an element of truth to it. There are, for me, films that depict things in truthful and believable ways, and then there is everything else. Just as I don't like lies in real life, I don't like them in art. It doesn't matter if a film is shot on 70mm or with a tiny camcorder, or if a story is the product of a wild imagination or from start to finish meticulously represents real events. What's important is that audiences can believe in it.

※ ※ ※

Cinema is nothing but fakery. It never depicts the truth as it actually is. A documentary, as I understand the word, is a film made by someone who doesn't intrude a single inch into what he is witness to. He merely records. A true documentary doesn't exist because reality isn't a sufficient foundation on which to construct an entire film. Filmmaking always involves some element of reinvention. Every story contains some level of fabrication because it bears the imprint of the person who made it. It reflects a point of view. Using a wide camera lens for a swooping twenty-second shot rather than a narrow lens for a static five-second shot reflects the filmmaker's biases. Colour or monochrome? Sound or silent? These decisions require that the filmmaker interfere in the process of representation.

A film can create a wildly unreal situation out of commonplace reality yet remain wedded to the truth. This is the essence of art. An animated film can never be real, but it might still be truthful. Two minutes into an outlandish science fiction film, full of believable characters in convincing situations, we forget it's all fantasy. We believe in a theatre actor who is lying dead on stage one minute and the very next stands before us taking a bow, receiving applause. Or when a character explains he is going on a long journey, then proceeds to take a stroll from one end of the stage to the other. Or when he is forced to break off suddenly from the action so he can flatten out his sword, which is made of soft metal and has become crooked during the performance. We comprehend that an actor can "die" on one stage, in one film, then appear again elsewhere, as someone else.

A film doesn't have to represent literal truth. Rather, truth can be emphasised. It can be accentuated and refined through interventions and intrusions, as we take control of a situation and represent it to the audience in creative ways. Allowing and encouraging that creativity is part of the contract an audience enters into with a filmmaker.

The final sequence of my film *Five* was shot at night, at a lagoon, two hundred and fifty miles from Tehran. There were only two nights every month and only two hours a night when the moon was as I wanted it, so though it looks like a single take of fifteen minutes, *Five* is actually comprised of hundreds of shots and took a year to make. Sometimes I made the drive but it was too cloudy or rainy, so I had to wait a month for my next chance. When the moon departs and goes behind a cloud, it does so in May, then reveals itself again in December. For most viewers the cuts and edits are unnoticeable. The soundtrack was also intricately pieced together. The serenading chorus of frogs, calling for the moon's return, even includes a soloist. The backup singers follow his lead.

I made a seventeen-minute film called *Seagull Eggs*, which appears to be a single-shot, real-time documentary. The image is of three eggs sitting precariously on a rock ledge, as waves crash around. We watch the frenzied movement of the water as it continuously engulfs the eggs, then retreats. Will the eggs survive the encounter or drop into the ocean, never to be seen again? After a few minutes, one of them disappears. Is the ocean satiated? Will it devour another? We wait attentively. Eventually a second egg disappears, then the third. Music swells on the soundtrack. End.

People tell me how wondrous it is that I happened upon this spot at just that particular moment, set down my camera and tripod, and started filming, presumably hoping that something interesting would happen. The truth is I assumed full control, starting with the eggs, which are goose eggs, bought from my local market because they are easier to find than seagull eggs. Each time one falls away, we hear the painful shrieks of birds, which creates a sense of anxiety. All these sounds were recorded separately and mixed together. I had about eight hours of footage in total, collected over two days. On day one, the sea was relatively calm. On the second, it was stormy, constantly buffeting the shore. In reality, it took only two minutes for all three eggs to be swept away. Again and again, my assistant kept replacing them and each time they disappeared within seconds. I spent four months editing *Seagull Eggs*, which is comprised of about twenty separate pieces of film. The idea came to me during a workshop not unlike this one.

Life and Nothing More is about a film director returning to an area of Iran where he made a film several years before, and that has recently suffered an earthquake. The film is set three days after the quake but was filmed months later, once much of the debris had been removed and tent cities established. When I asked people who had lived through the catastrophe to put into disarray the few possessions they had salvaged, to make the landscape look more like it had done a few months previously, many refused. Amid the ruin and destruction, they began washing rugs and hanging them on trees to dry, and some borrowed new clothes to wear for the filming. Their instinct for survival was powerful, as was their desire to maintain self-respect in the midst of such harsh circumstances. They wanted to put on a show that didn't match the reality I was hoping to capture. Like several of my films, *Life and Nothing More* is simultaneously a documentary and a work of fiction.

There is a similar to-and-fro between fantasy and reality in *Close-Up*. For the trial scene, I planned on having three cameras inside the real-life courtroom. One was for a close-up of the defendant Hossein Sabzian, the second for a wider shot of the courtroom, the third to emphasise the relationship between Sabzian and the judge. Almost immediately, one of the cameras broke and another was so noisy I was forced to turn it off. We ended up having to move our single workable camera from one spot to the next, which meant missing a continuous shot of Sabzian. This is why, when the trial ended after only one hour and the judge left because he was so busy, we filmed with Sabzian, behind closed doors, for another nine hours. I talked with him and suggested what he might say on camera. We ended up recreating most of the trial in the judge's absence. The occasional shots of him that I inserted into *Close-Up*, to make it seem as if he had been present the whole time, constitute one of the biggest lies in any of my films.

While these films are packed with artifice – like so much of my cinema, which appears to be a reflection of reality though is actually often something quite different – they are all wholly believable. Everything is lies, nothing is real, and yet it all suggests the truth. Whether I agree with or approve of something in a story is secondary to whether I believe it. I lose contact with a film I don't believe in. I fell asleep before the ending of the first Hollywood film I ever saw, and even as a child felt that the fictional characters in the story had nothing to do with real life, with me. My work consists of telling lies in such a way that people believe them. I furnish audiences with falsehoods, but do so persuasively. Every filmmaker has his own interpretation of reality, which makes every filmmaker a liar. But these lies serve to express a sort of profound human truth.

❀ ❀ ❀

There is nothing particularly important about realism. Its value comes from how we interpret and represent. Truth isn't the opposite of lying, it's the discovery of the unknown. Truth and revelation will always be more important than realism.

❀ ❀ ❀

An exact imitation of life, if such a thing is even possible, cannot be art. Some measure of control is necessary, otherwise the filmmaker is little more than a surveillance camera in the corner of a room or a camera affixed to the horns of a bull in a field, blindly recording. But even then, which room and which bull? Choices must be made, and by so doing essential truths are revealed.

consists of telling lies in such a way that people believe them. I furnish audiences with falsehoods, but do so persuasively. Every

❁ ❁ ❁

Does an audience need to understand that certain things in my films appear to be one thing but are actually something else? Are the details of production important? I don't think so. It's no one's business but my own to know precisely how things are done. All the audience need do is watch and discover some truthfulness in the images, to believe what I am showing them. Perhaps I should avoid revealing too many details because – even if during these highly technological days we can't always completely trust what we are looking at – people tend to believe what they see. More than once someone has implored me to stop sharing the specifics of how my films are made. Most people, it seems, don't want to know, just as they would prefer never to see their favourite actors without makeup. They don't want to see what goes on behind the curtain. But telling you about the two days I filmed those eggs sitting on that rock ledge, or the judge leaving the courtroom after an hour because he had other things to do, ultimately doesn't much matter. The films are still enjoyable and meaningful. You here, in this room, probably notice the fabrications in my work quicker than the average viewer. If a filmmaker told me there was a lie in his work and I couldn't work out what it was, I would congratulate him.

❁ ❁ ❁

An exhibition of landscapes. Balzac and the artist stand before a canvas. In the background of this painting, far from the main action, is a small house in the middle of the field. Smoke rises from the chimney. There is life here. Balzac turns to the painter. "How many people live in the house?" he asks.

"I don't know. Maybe six or seven."

"You mean a family?"

"Perhaps. Yes, a family."

"How many children?"

The painter thinks. "Three," he announces.

"How old are they?"

Hmm... Maybe eight, ten and twelve."

The conversation continues in this vein until the painter, somewhat frustrated, says, "Mr. Balzac, it's just a tiny house in the background of the picture. It doesn't matter how many people live there. I don't know all these details."

"I know you don't care about things like this," says Balzac. "It's clear to me you don't know how many children live there and how many roosters are in the front yard and what Mother is preparing for supper and whether Father can afford his eldest daughter's dowry. I know this because I see smoke coming from the chimney, but I don't believe it. It doesn't look real to me. Had you known these things, it would be a better painting."

As filmmakers you need to know these kinds of details, about what is taking place outside the frame, even though no one will ever see it. To have these facts at your fingertips – how harsh was last year's winter? what crops grow behind the house? what tragedies have struck this family of late? – will make your ideas more compelling and the performances you coax from your actors more detailed and believable. These days, before I write anything down, I have approximate images of certain things in my head, as if I am watching the film before I have made it. I can visualise the characters living in that landscape. For several of my films, I selected the actors long before we started shooting. Sometimes I lived with these people and got to know them as best I could, developing the script in tandem with this knowledge. Spending time with an actor, sometimes for months before filming, means I could write an entire novel about him and the character he is going to play. It's an invaluable process, though I would never share most of that information with the actor playing the part. It's unlikely to help him one bit when he steps in front of the camera.

Constructing a story in this way, from the inside, and including in a film certain intimate details, amounts to a richer, deeper experience for audiences. They notice the difference. With time to work only on four- or five-minute-long films this week, rid yourself of complex ideas, of detailed philosophy and psychology, of convoluted backstory. When it comes to filmmaking, as with anything, a certain discipline is required to develop the requisite simplicity. When you start work on your films, keep the storytelling straightforward and self-contained. In a four-minute film, you don't have time to explore anyone's past in detail. The most important thing is what the audience sees and hears. Whatever the characters want, whatever they are doing, needs to be represented physically, in human gestures. Let's start thinking cinematically, in images. When you tell your story to the group, don't philosophise. Explain nothing. Just describe what we see and hear. A filmmaker doesn't hand out a written manifesto to an audience before it watches his work.

11

❂❂❂

I want to help you find beauty in the prosaic. I want to help you look anew and move beyond your conventional way of seeing things. This week we will cleanse our eyes together. We will re-educate ourselves together.

❂❂❂

There is a sort of cinema – widespread today – that doesn't require an audience to exercise its imagination. After all, it's not difficult to manipulate someone's emotions. Bad films nail you to your seat. They take you hostage. Everything is up there on the screen, but everything is closed off to interpretation, with the director dictating precisely how you should be feeling. Then, within a few minutes of the lights coming up, you have forgotten everything and feel cheated.

I prefer a different sort of cinema. When audiences – so vulnerable sitting in a darkened auditorium – aren't being robbed of their reason and subjected to this emotional blackmail, they look at things with a more mindful eye. A good film stops you in your tracks. It provokes, awakening something within, working you over long after it has ended. A good film needs to be completed by me, in my head, sometimes much later. It can put me to sleep while I watch, but weeks later I might awake, fired up, imagination running wild, and say to myself, "I need to look at that again." I don't mind if someone dozes off while watching one of my films, so long as they dream about it later.

"I couldn't put it down!" is what you hear people say about their experiences of reading a book. Why is that a good thing? Great art inspires, thereby requiring some sort of intervention. It's too stimulating to be experienced in one go. Some films force me to switch off and head to the kitchen for a drink, or just stand before a window and stare. There is so much to think about that I have to remove myself and take a break. Back in the day, when I used to watch films, often I would leave after a particularly impressive or moving sequence, or even after a single, startling image had flashed before my eyes. I already had my own ending in mind and suspected that my conclusion to the story was more interesting than the actual one. In some cases the film up to that point was sufficient. I just didn't need to see anything more. I needed distance, if only for a few minutes. Sometimes, when editing a film, I want to cut to a completely empty, soundless screen for five minutes. The effect would be like the blank page of a novel that allows the reader a moment to pause and ponder. But I can never quite muster the nerve.

❀ ❀ ❀

Decades ago I was at a film festival in France, where my film *The Experience* was screened. It was an important moment for me because finally I had the chance to show my work outside my own country. In the middle of the screening the doors crashed open and a group carrying placards crowded inside. We had been invaded by a political demonstration. The projector was turned off and the lights came on. I exited quickly, downhearted because I had so enjoyed watching my film with this audience, then noticed that it was being screened in another auditorium across town, so I dashed over there. I found an empty front row seat in the darkness and sat down. "Everyone is dead quiet. They must be absolutely entranced by the film," I thought to myself. When the lights came up, I turned around. All four members of the audience were fast asleep.

❀ ❀ ❀

A few years ago, at a screening of a couple of my films, somewhere in Europe, an employee of the local Iranian embassy said to me, "You're a fine filmmaker, Mr. Kiarostami, but you have a long way to go before you make a film as good as *Ben-Hur*."

❀ ❀ ❀

If God has provided us with one thing, it's the power of imagination. Dreaming clearly has some function, otherwise why would we be capable of it? The ugliness of the world lies before us, whether we want to look or not, but as we filter things and dig into our inhibitions, as we dream and fantasise, we come to learn about our true feelings and beliefs and desires. By doing so, we temporarily escape real life.

Some people need their imagination more than others. When things are difficult we automatically begin dreaming. The more we reject reality, the more we take refuge in our imagination, which only we have command of, which no system of inquisition can control. With dreams we cut through the dreariness of life, even pass through prison walls, all without moving an inch. Dreaming is an opportunity to make life more tolerable. It provides us with a more powerful level of resilience, of acceptance of certain hardships. If there were a machine that could measure our dream life, we would discover that the imaginations of subway workers are perpetually fired up because they spend all day in the darkness of the underworld. Birds sing loudest when held captive in a cage.

Dreams refresh. Inside a room and in need of air, you open a window. Or think of a heating system in a house that automatically clicks on when the temperature drops too low. Someone once asked me if I had to lose either my eyes or my dream life, which would it be? "I'll keep my eyes," I said, but then realised that blindness is bearable compared to not being able to dream, that dreaming is one of humankind's most wondrous abilities. We appreciate our capacity for sight and hearing and smell and touch, but what would life be if we couldn't dream? The value of something goes unnoticed until it has vanished. This week, if anyone finds what is being said in this room boring, tune out and start dreaming. Move beyond your usual way of thinking.

They say an artist paints what he sees, that you should make films about what you know. I can't think of worse advice for a filmmaker. It's true that real life is often the foundation of my stories and the impetus for my films, that everyday people walking in the street inspire me. I don't invent so much as stay on the alert, focused on what is around me, then provoke and organise things as they play out in front of the camera. I am like a florist who doesn't grow flowers, only arranges them. Filmmakers who peruse books and magazines for stories to tell are like people who live near a fast-flowing stream full of plump, healthy fish, yet eat out of sardine cans.

But though I allow the world to permeate me, though I get ideas from the people around me, the best storytelling is inspired by dreams and imagination, by being removed from the literal world. Most people don't appreciate the possibilities offered to them by their imagination, which at its most powerful can subdue and outshine everything. As a starting point, always go to the source of things: life itself. Explore first what lies around you. But then move beyond. The ideal arrangement is to be in perpetual motion between reality and dreamland, between the world and imagination. Reality stimulates creativity, but cinema

moves us beyond daily life, offering a window onto our dreams. Therein lies its potential. A poet – I don't know who – said art is the interweaving of rationality and emotion. Neither reason nor real life alone have ever been sufficient.

✹ ✹ ✹

Communal experiences are important. Being able to exist within a crowd is a good indication that someone could, if need be, exist on their own. Confront your personal fears and you will likely be able to confront collective fears. At the same time, everyone naturally thinks differently. Within every group you find a multitude of particular reactions and unique interpretations, all connected yet separate. Each person's imagination yields uniquely, and surrendering to group interests undermines individuality. We are all affected in singular ways. It is perilous to suppress such things. Education might be the key to society's problems, but it can also suffocate, erase personality, and crush the imagination. Knowledge for its own sake isn't useful. It has to be personalised. Collective thinking troubles me.

✹ ✹ ✹

While editing the sequence in *The Experience* of the boy hanging his socks out to dry, I discovered continuity issues. We had forgotten to leave the socks hanging on the line. They were in one shot, but vanished in the next. I was upset, even more so when the owner of the shop where we filmed refused to let us back to re-shoot. I sat next to a friend during the first screening of the film, and when the scene came up I started talking so as to distract him. I didn't want him to notice those missing socks. As I left the cinema, I expected to hear people complaining about the socks and was genuinely surprised that no one seemed to notice. If you can hook an audience with a compelling story, certain details become inconsequential.

✹ ✹ ✹

Unlike in the West, where poetry is primarily the domain of elites, there are illiterate Iranians who have committed lengthy passages of verse to memory. It's a country where we decorate the graves of poets, where there are television channels that do nothing but broadcast the recitation of poetry. Whenever my grandmother wanted to complain or express her love for something, she did so using poetry. Relatively simple folk in Iran carry with them a philosophy of life which is poetic in its expression. When it comes to filmmaking, this is the treasure that compensates for our technical shortcomings.

I was once asked if the basis of Iranian art is poetry. I said that the basis of all art is poetry. Art is about revelation, about new information being rendered. True poetry, similarly, elevates us to the sublime. It overturns and helps us escape our habitual, familiar and mechanical routines, which is the first step towards discovery and breakthrough. It exposes a world otherwise concealed from the human eye. It goes beyond reality, deep into the realm of truth, and enables us to fly one thousand feet up and look down upon the world. Anything else is not poetry. With no art, with no poetry, comes impoverishment.

The novels I own are in near-perfect condition because I read them once then put them aside, but the poetry books on my shelves are falling apart at the seams. I return to them continually. Poetry isn't easy to grasp because instead of being told a story, we are presented with a series of abstractions. The essence of poetry is a level of incomprehension. A poem, by its very nature, is unfinished and unfixed. It invites us to complete it, to fill in the blanks, to join the dots. Crack the code and the mysteries reveal themselves. True poetry will always outlive mere storytelling.

A poem appears different at every reading, depending on your state of mind and stage of life. It grows and changes alongside you, perhaps even within you. This is why the poems I read as a child yield different experiences for me today. A poem that yesterday edified might tomorrow seem tedious. Or, perhaps, with a new outlook on life and a new understanding, I feel exhilaration in finding things I missed all those years ago. In any given situation, in any given period, we relate to poetry in a new way. Poems are like mirrors in which we rediscover ourselves.

As a young man – when I was perhaps fifteen or sixteen – I adored the work of Mehdi Hamidi Shirazi, his intense love poems, full of grief and loss. I couldn't afford his books, so my friend took a copy from his brother's room and lent it to me for three days and nights. It was crucial that it be put back on the shelf before his brother noticed. I spent that time writing out the entire book in longhand, and by doing so began to memorise the text. Much later, I became disenchanted with the fact that my head was full of all these verses and rhythms. Just as some people come to dislike the fading tattoos on their body, I resented that my head was packed with such vivid poetry that no longer had the same meaning for me. Later again I travelled to London with a friend, who told me he wanted me to meet someone. "You won't have heard of him," my friend explained, "but he is a poet whose work has greatly touched me." It turned out to be Hamidi Shirazi. I remember wondering if it was a good idea that I go face to face with this man whose work had caused me such anxiety. My friend insisted, and we visited Hamidi Shirazi, who it turned out was deathly ill. "I am here with Mr. Kiarostami," my friend said. "He knows much of your poetry by heart. Would you like him to recite something for you?" Hamidi Shirazi nodded. The most extraordinary thing happened as I began to speak his lines. The poet wept, and my friend was similarly moved to tears. Even I experienced intense feelings as I recited those verses, all those years after turning my back on them.

At that moment I realised my feat of memory had been far from useless, that it hadn't been a waste of time. I stood there, words pouring from my tongue, and returned the poetry to its author. At the same time I re-engaged with it myself. My feelings about life had changed, and so had my feelings about Hamidi Shirazi's work. How could it be otherwise?

Who faults a poem because he doesn't understand it? What does it even mean to "understand" a poem? Do we understand a piece of music? Do we understand an abstract painting? We all have our own comprehension of things, our own threshold where understanding blurs, at which point perplexity sets in. With poetry, an immediate and full understanding can't be expected. Such things have to be worked for. In the case of cinema, too many films spoon-feed. Audiences have been led to expect a constantly clear and unified message. They consume without thought, thereby conditioning themselves against films with open endings, against my kind of cinema. Too many inquisitive people seem to lose that curiosity after buying a ticket for a film. Out of habit they unquestionably accept what is offered to them – this overdose of information or order or explanation – and are uninterested in discovering things for themselves. They want to be able to look at a film straight on and understand it immediately and fully. If a single moment is obscure, the entire film becomes mystifying.

I like my half-finished cinema to be vague. I like ambiguities. I am a filmmaker who asks audiences to make more effort than usual, to bask in temporary confusion, and by so doing express themselves, which is why I lose some viewers along the way. For me, film is about enticing people to look and ask questions, to take the trouble to consider cinema as something other than just entertainment.

If a story is missing its final page, we are forced to guess what happened to our hero, what decisions he made. It's as if the author is letting his readers complete the story themselves. At the end of my film *The Report*, a couple with marital problems is in a hospital room. She has attempted suicide and is in bed. He is on a chair next to her, where he sits throughout the night. The next morning he sees that his wife's eyes are open, that she is alive. He picks up his jacket and leaves. The last shot of the film is of the hospital's front doors as this man walks out, gets into his car, and drives away. An ending like that gives me the opportunity to avoid answering questions and, instead, pose them. The audience is forced to make up its own mind about what happens to these two people. A film with an open ending is more believable than one with a definitive, solid and sealed-off resolution. What film starts at the beginning of a character's life and ends with the end of that life? Everyone has a past and future we never see. This workshop will finish and we will all go home, but the ideas we have been talking about will continue to work us over. There is no definitive closure to our experiences here this week. A story starts before we encounter it and concludes long after we have turned away.

When I talk of poetic cinema, I am thinking about the kind of cinema that possesses the qualities of poetry, that encompasses the vast potential of poetic language. It has the capabilities of a prism. It has a complexity to it. It has a lasting quality. It's like an unfinished puzzle that invites us to decipher the message and put the pieces together in whatever arrangement we want.

Audiences are used to films that offer clear and definite endings, but a film with a poetic essence has a certain ambiguity and can be looked at in many different ways. It allows for fantasies to develop in the viewer's imagination. Alternative interpretations thrive. A poem asks us to discover its meaning by combining subjective feelings and ideas with the feelings and ideas on the page, which means our understanding is very much our own. If it weren't for the subconscious, much of what we consider art would be unsuccessful. What happens between the lines of a poem occurs in only one place: inside our heads. Why can't cinema be the same? If a level of incomprehension is inherent in poetry, why can't it be so with cinema? Why can't a film be experienced like a poem, an abstract painting, or a piece of music? Cinema will never be considered a major art form unless the possibility of incomprehension is accepted as a positive attribute.

❊ ❊ ❊

Someone from outside Iran with no understanding of Persian poetry can appreciate my work because poetry is a state of mind. An understanding of poetry from one culture means an understanding of all poetry. There is a universality.

❊ ❊ ❊

Poetry can be an ambiguous form of expression in which certain ideas you might not otherwise talk about in public can be concealed and explored. Why not film, too?

❊ ❊ ❊

How much can you make visible without actually showing anything? I want to create the kind of cinema that shows by not showing. Some films reveal so much that there is no space for the audience's imagination to intervene. My aim is to allow whoever is watching to create as much as possible in his own mind. As we watch the characters in a film and explore the situations they find themselves in, we are reminded of the sweetness and bitterness, accord and strife, folly and wisdom of our own lives. Cinema intrigues as much because of the feelings and thoughts it causes to flow through the minds of viewers as what is actually playing out on the screen before their eyes. I want everyone to watch my films with their own interpretations working in tandem. I want to tap the hidden information within that you probably didn't even know was there. When somebody is looking with real intensity, in Persian we say: "He had two eyes and borrowed two more." Those two borrowed eyes are what I want to bring to life. They enable us to see what is happening beyond the image itself.

❀ ❀ ❀

There is scant dignity in the kind of cinema that allows only one version of reality. A director who wants his work received uniformly by audiences is guilty of ignoring his audience's potential. Individualism and difference of opinion are what I want from those who watch my films. Unanimous opinions are tiresome.

A poetic film is made once by the director and then again in the viewer's mind, which is why I have no interest in explaining anything. If an audience sees one of my films and interprets it in ways I didn't intend, then we all benefit when I keep my mouth shut. Once a film has been completed, its creator should get out of the way. Self-respecting viewers will turn away from what I say about my work because everyone brings themselves to a film. They infuse their own ideas, beliefs, joys and dislikes with the characters and colours they are looking at, the voices and sounds they are listening to. By doing so, they complete the film. Most audiences have fiendishly fertile and creative imaginations, which means I don't have to do all the work.

❀ ❀ ❀

In *Through the Olive Trees* there is an argument between a character in a car and some labourers whose equipment is blocking the way. We experience the incident only through the faces of those involved, and never see the road, yet nonetheless feel we

21

have been shown everything. Our mind is awash with images of that blocked road. Picture a scene in a film where we cut back and forth between two people speaking to each other by telephone. Compare this to a scene where we hear the exact same dialogue, but see only one of the speakers. In fact, consider a third option: we hear every word being said but see neither of the people talking. We behold something wholly other, something that is, at first glance, completely disconnected from the conversation of these two people. Such juxtapositions can be provocative. Why not let the audience do some work?

In *Taste of Cherry* we follow Badii, a middle-aged man, whose plan is to swallow sleeping pills and then lie in a ditch by the side of the road on the outskirts of Tehran. He is searching for someone to assist with his suicide, someone who will cover him over with earth the following morning. By the end of the film we haven't discovered if he has been successful in his task. People ask me if Badii is dead and complain that it's unclear why he even wants to commit suicide. As far as I'm concerned, audiences don't need to know exactly what his troubles are, they just need to know that this man is in distress. It's up to them to determine the specifics. After a screening in New York, a woman told me that Badii is most definitely unhappy in love, while her husband insisted that the cause of his problems is the borrowed money he is unable to repay. Divergent reactions like these reveal more about the life of that couple than my film ever could about Badii. Some people tell me *Taste of Cherry* is optimistic and lighthearted, some say it's pessimistic and sinister. One person even told me it's erotic. These are all valid points of view I can understand.

I published a book of photographs, called *Rain and Wind*, which is comprised entirely of images shot from inside moving cars, through rain-spattered windows. I took some of them with the camera in one hand, the other on the steering wheel. In none of these images is the world outside entirely clear to see. Presumably everyone looks at these photographs of obscured pieces of glass differently. It's a sort of Rorschach test. We all find something unique – the outline of a road, landscape, car, tree or building – to consider. Another book of my photos contains images of walls, yet another of beautiful old doors, always closed, and still another of windows. The simple question is the always the same: what lies beyond? I am inviting you to look behind the curtain.

In *Ten*, which was shot in a car driving through Tehran, the camera shows Mania Akbari's face as she watches the traffic around her, which we never see. It's more interesting if we allow the audience to imagine everything itself. What sort of car just pulled out in front of her? Who is driving? Is there anyone in the passenger seat? Where are they going? These are questions I could never answer, and never felt the need to answer. At the start of the film, Mania's son is sitting next to her in the car. The scenes in which we catch a brief, distant glimpse of his father, and for a few seconds hear how the two of them talk with each other, are enough to suggest the ways in which the child resembles this man. Nothing more is needed to represent the patriarchal society in which they live and how this impacts the boy's relationship with his mother.

There were two cameras in the car, but I decided to stay fixed on the boy for the first sixteen minutes of the film. By withholding a view of the mother – we only hear her voice – audiences become increasingly curious about who she is, what she looks like. The child gave a startlingly compelling performance because he was so sublimely believable. Even so, we can't get this woman out of our

23

minds, or the desire to see her. Because she is faceless, unseen, for those sixteen minutes, every woman is able to imagine herself as the mother of this petulant young man.

❁ ❁ ❁

I have never wanted everyone to watch a film as if they were doing a crossword puzzle, where answers are the same for everybody. The identity of a film is established by whoever is watching it, which means there are as many meanings as there are members of the audience. A film shouldn't have a solid structure or a clear-cut conclusion. There should be holes and fissures into which the audience can climb. It's a never-ending game. I encourage you to leave things unsaid as much as possible. When something is definitely stated, there is no room for maneuver. Inject ambiguity, and an audience feels boundless. Take advantage of opportunities to withhold details, and viewers are empowered. The moment someone sees one of my films, something new has been created. The more open-ended a film, the more interpretations are inspired. As Rumi tells us, "Everyone becomes my friend by virtue of his own vision."

❁ ❁ ❁

It wouldn't be right if all a film director did was talk and all the audience did was listen. I don't have any answers for viewers. It's up to them to respond and reflect in their own ways. We filmmakers may have access to cameras and be in charge of editing, but that doesn't mean everyone else is any less creative or even in less control of determining the meaning of a film. When a filmmaker pulls back the curtain, every member of the audience – their imaginations enriched – creates his own world. Although I rarely hear the details of such things, as a filmmaker I still rely on that creativity. More than anything else, a film should be an *aide-mémoire*. Every member of the audience should be able to connect a film to his own fears and passions. Films that don't allow this sort of intervention, that can be described in twenty words or less, aren't what I want to see. The more a film is committed to having a beginning, middle and end, the more resistant I am. The age of Scheherazade – of audiences being held in suspense, of knowing within the first five shots of a film who the hero is, what his motives are, how difficult his goal is, what obstacles are in his way, who will be there to assist him, and being certain that he will prevail – needs to end.

❀ ❀ ❀

If you are sincere when you make a film, if you don't think exclusively about the requirements of the marketplace, your work will contain elements of your personality whether you intend it or not.

❀ ❀ ❀

Some of the most interesting films made at workshops come from those participants with the least technical ability and using the fewest tools, but always exercising a maximum of effort.

❀ ❀ ❀

Painful it is when a single person – an artist or a politician – decides something on behalf of everyone else. The job of the artist is to bring problems to light, but everybody has a responsibility to contemplate them. The director and audience are equals, on the same footing. Year ago, emerging from a screening of one of my films, I was applauded. So I applauded back.

❀ ❀ ❀

The cameraman of *Through the Olive Trees* complained about not being able to see the faces of the two main characters because they were so far from the camera. He wanted to shoot a close-up. I told him it wasn't necessary, that each member of the audience would do that in their own minds if they wanted to. When presented with intriguing characters in intriguing situations, no matter how far from the camera, perceptive viewers will work things out for themselves.

Some cameramen are like police mug shot photographers, insisting that both ears be visible at all times. A more respectful approach is to avoid directing the audience's eye so explicitly. Allow people to decide for themselves what to zoom in on and look at. Even the best television commercials I saw last night in my hotel room, in between *The Godfather* – a film I admire, by the way – are made this way. "A book read by one thousand different people," said Andrei Tarkovsky, "is one thousand different books." The power of art resides in the different responses it creates in different people. Although I'm not particularly fond of his films, I find Robert Bresson's theories interesting, especially his method of creation through omission. "One does not create by adding but by taking away," he wrote. There are some things that don't need to be seen. My way of framing a shot is to force the viewer to sit with his back straight, stretching his neck, looking for whatever is not showing.

Someone can make an impact on us through her absence. The funeral ceremony that the story of *The Wind Will Carry Us* revolves around is never shown, but every member of the audience still has his own sense of what it looks like. Several characters are only talked about, never seen, but by the end of the film we feel as if they were there all along. Each of us imagines these missing people in our own way, and by so doing actively participates in the film's creation. Every unseen character has as many faces as there are members of the audience. The more creative the filmmaker is in removing information from the screen, the more interested audiences become. Their minds ignite. They don't even need a director.

In *Certified Copy* we see the child only at the beginning of the film, but his presence is evident throughout, like a cross his mother has to bear. In *Taste of Cherry* Badii's family is unseen, but I felt there was at all times a particular woman, implicit, hiding in the background of the film, and therefore also in the mind of the audience. The fact that we never see her doesn't prevent us from formulating an idea of the relationship between these two people. That emptiness is almost a means of attributing even greater importance to her. When we see Badii through the window of his apartment, we wonder where his wife and children are. When we look through our neighbour's window and notice someone inside, or sit across from an elderly couple in a restaurant, we imagine their entire lives. We hear only fragments of their conversation, yet complete stories and vivid scenes flash across our minds.

I made a film called *Close-Up*, about a real man named Hossein Sabzian – a great lover of cinema – who convinces the prosperous Ahankhan family in Tehran that he is the famous Iranian film director Mohsen Makhmalbaf and will one day put them in one of his films. The family invites Sabzian into their home and lends him money before realising the truth and turning him over to the police. At the end of the film, we see Sabzian leaving prison and meeting the real Makhmalbaf for the first time. Sabzian embraces Makhmalbaf with great emotion and they ride off together on a motorbike.

I was following in a car, listening to them talking, and quickly realised that nothing they were saying would fit in the film. The problem was that Makhmalbaf knew he was being recorded but Sabzian didn't. It was just two opposing monologues rather than a dialogue I could use. The fake director was too real and the real director was too fake. What's more, we were wrapping up production, and leaving in unedited dialogue between the two of them would have shifted the film in a new direction. The narrative had to be progressively directed towards a climax, not opened up. The dialogue as spoken would also have made Makhmalbaf the hero, but I wanted Sabzian to be at the story's centre from start to finish. Anything else and *Close-Up* would have become unbalanced, like Marlon Brando showing up for the first time in the final ten minutes of a film.

I was up all night wondering how to make the sequence work before realising the solution was to make it seem as if the microphone was faulty. The editor looked at me in disbelief when I told him I wanted to slice up the recording. He outright refused to involve himself with such lunacy, so I did it myself. You hear an audible word only here and there during that scene. Everything else is beyond comprehension. Today I consider it one of the most important moments in any of my films, especially whenever anyone complains because they want to know what Makhmalbaf and Sabzian are saying to each other. The audience has been primed, pushed to think about things beyond the frame of the film. They want to know what lies off-screen, which means they have to fill in the gaps themselves.

◎◎◎

I wonder if I could ever do what Sabzian did. Who is completely happy with themselves? Don't we all sometimes imagine what it would be like to be someone else? There is a Sabzian hiding inside us all. When I was sixteen, I copied *The Songs of Bilitis* for a girl, telling her I had written it. Each of us hunts for a different identity.

For me, *Close-Up* is about the power of love. When someone adores something so intensely – cinema, in this case – he is capable of amazing boldness. Able to tell such spectacular lies to the Ahankhan family, Sabzian transformed himself into a genuine artist. When I went to the family home to stage the scene where Sabzian is arrested, he told one of the sons that he had not, in fact, played a trick on them. At long last here he was, keeping his promise to bring a camera crew with him. The family would be in a film after all. Were we the crew that Sabzian had dreamed of? I was dumbstruck. What Sabzian said to the Ahankhans might have been a part of his fantasy, but it was somehow also true because the family ended up playing a version of themselves in *Close-Up*. Cinema has the wondrous power of fulfilling our wishes to be somebody else.

◎◎◎

There is a scene in *Taste of Cherry* set at the natural history museum in Tehran. Badii looks through the window into a room where students are dissecting quails. We hear them talking with their teacher but see nothing. No scalpel or birds, no teacher or

28

students. All we experience are noises and fragments of dialogue that enable us to visualise what is going on. Sometimes the sight of someone's feet is the best indication of his state of mind. Rumi advises that those who want to see better should open the eyes of their heart.

❀ ❀ ❀

Films that contain good ideas are always worth something, even if they aren't well made. An uninteresting idea is like a piece of cracked glass or stagnant water. It just sits, offering nothing.

❀ ❀ ❀

After a screening of *Certified Copy*, someone asked about my use of reflections in the film, about windows and mirrors. After a question like that I start quietly criticising myself. "If I had known such things would be so apparent," I said to the audience, "I would have used fewer of them." I don't consciously add symbolism to my films. A filmmaker can use a symbol to relay his intentions, but why not consider drawing from a much richer realm, from the very source of symbolism itself? Reality is so overflowing, so compelling, that there seems to be little point in representing things allegorically. Just point the camera, face on, at the world. There is something authoritarian and rigid in symbolism, with the creator conveying his direct intentions, insisting we consider something in a specific way. It doesn't allow room for us to interpret things ourselves, to make them our own. As for those people who seem to find symbols in every corner of my films, let them enjoy the search. It does no harm, and occasionally even teaches me something.

❀ ❀ ❀

Sound and image should ideally be separate elements. As a filmmaker, consider them independent of each other. Just as an image shouldn't require a sound to make it comprehensible, neither should an audience need an image in order to understand a particular sound. The aesthetics of cinema are rooted in the separation of what we hear and what we see.

❀ ❀ ❀

29

Sound can be an effective mechanism for suggesting the presence of things we do not see, for giving an image a third dimension. Picture a scene in which we hear the noise of a motorcycle, then the screech of it braking and crashing. Two women arrive at the accident site. The camera holds only on them, with the crashed motorcycle out of frame, but from their reactions the audience perceives the seriousness of the situation. Each of us involuntarily brings to mind an image of what just happened on that street corner. When sound fills in what is unseen, giving an image more depth, the filmmaker is able to show even less. In a film set in the city, a car horn and the sound of metal striking metal, followed by the reaction of a witness to this event, is all the information we need. Sounds set the mind going by arousing us, sometimes in cunning ways. In *Close-Up*, when Sabzian sits in the bus and signs Makhmalbaf's book as if he wrote it himself, we hear a siren in the background, suggesting that something isn't quite right. When someone is arrested in *Fellow Citizen*, we hear a flock of crows, which for Iranians is the bearer of bad news.

As we go about our lives, we often take into account only one dimension, only one side of the cube, oblivious to the fact that there are five others. But listen carefully. Some people are talking at the back of the room. There are cars driving around outside. The lights above us are buzzing. From the corner comes the ticking of a clock. A woman taps her finger on a desk. With five carefully placed sounds, an audience has five new and different opportunities to comprehend a scene. The storytelling experience is enriched. Before heading off to make a film, my joke to the cameraman is that we are going out to record a few sounds, but he may as well bring his camera along to capture some images here and there. I once visited a gallery in New York where the artist had made the most of every inch of exhibition space, where the walls, doors, ceiling and floor were all skilfully integrated. I felt surrounded on all sides by the experience he had created, by that complete environment he had constructed. It's what I hope to achieve with my films. I point the camera at something and show audiences only one side of the cube, a single image within the frame, but by exploiting the capabilities of cinema – of the medium – I can ensure that audiences are imagining the other five.

◈ ◈ ◈

I participated in the *Lumière et compagnie* project, which involved using the original Lumière camera, with reels lasting less than a minute, and without synchronised sound. My contribution was a single, fixed shot of a frying pan full of sizzling butter, then an egg cracked open, followed by the pan – now containing a fried egg – being removed from the cooker. What drives the film beyond this dinner-for-one is the soundtrack, which documents a dying relationship. We hear a woman leaving a phone message on a machine. "It's me," she says. "Are you there? Hello? Hello? Well, I'm here... I'm not going anywhere. Bye." I asked Isabelle Huppert to call me at home and talk into my answering machine.

❀ ❀ ❀

As a child I would spend hours listening to the radio in the darkness, visualising what I was hearing. It really set my imagination to work. Sixty years later, I can still see the things I heard on the radio. A film that so inflames our imagination is a work of true creativity.

❀ ❀ ❀

It takes a certain audacity – courage, even – to put emptiness on screen, to show nothing. That courage comes from faith I have in the viewer.

❀ ❀ ❀

There is no key I can supply to an audience and thereby help unlock and decipher a film. And even if there were such a thing, I would deny all knowledge of it. A sense of wonder, even confusion, is what the filmmaker should be aiming for.

❀ ❀ ❀

You may not always have good luck when making a film, but pay attention, keep an open mind, and be flexible. You might be able to turn bad luck into good. Renoir said that if a drop of paint accidentally falls onto a canvas, the painting isn't necessarily ruined. Create a new composition instead. I remember turning an

31

inadvertent smudge in one of my own paintings into a chair. Today I look at that canvas and consider it much improved because of that chair. Mistakes and shortcomings can have a positive effect. The first time I showed *Close-Up* was in Munich. The projectionist got the reels in the wrong order, though I didn't say anything because I saw that his accidental version was better than mine. When I got home I re-edited the film and moved the scene of the meeting in the bus – which was originally at the start of the film – to the middle of the trial.

An ability to respond creatively to calamities, which occur so often, is what impresses me, not technical virtuosity. Hafez advises that accidental events can be of value. Make the most of chance and the unforeseen. Cherish the incidental. Embrace the accidental.

❀ ❀

The camera is like a pen. To become a good calligrapher you must write and write. If you want to develop an eye, look and look, then pick up a camera. My grandmother would sit in the back seat of the car and say, "Look at that tree, that hill, that mountain." She was showing me unexpected things among all those images and angles. She had made her own choices and was enjoying them. My grandmother had the mind of a filmmaker.

❀ ❀

What I put on film isn't as important as the image residing within.

❀ ❀

With 35mm film, the filmmaker has to be in control of everything and constantly intervene to fix what isn't right. But thanks to digital video, we can keep our distance while the actors do what they feel is necessary. Digital technology has profoundly changed the nature of filmmaking. I remember being excited about the fresh possibilities it brought, like a painter who has discovered a new colour. One hundred years ago, clothes were covered in buttons and laces, and it took hours to get dressed. The idea of just a shirt and a pair of jeans was out of the question. A similar revolution to the one that happened in clothing has taken place in cinema.

The best writers are probably the ones whose books we can find if we look hard enough, but the best filmmakers aren't necessarily those people who ever made a film. Until fairly recently, only people with access to expensive equipment could make films. Today, small, self-contained digital cameras have freed cinema from the clutches of capital, and telling a story in moving images isn't such an insurmountable obstacle. In the past, someone might have gone from one producer to the next, insisting they could prove themselves as a filmmaker of genius if only someone would give them enough money. A bus driver might be a great filmmaker but until recently never had access to equipment. Digital technology is a sieve that will filter out the truly skilled. We can finally solve the problem of all those wandering minds. Today these people have no excuses, just as you have no excuses this week, with all this equipment laid out before you, these resources at your disposal, this time on your hands. Don't let this opportunity slip away. The candle burns fast.

❀ ❀ ❀

My general method of filmmaking forty years ago, when I was shooting on 16mm film, wasn't much different to the way I do things today, when I might use a small hand-held video camera. We all have our own way of working, our own approach to storytelling, regardless of available tools.

❀ ❀ ❀

There are new technical possibilities emerging every day for the filmmaker. But don't feel obliged to use them all.

❀ ❀ ❀

I have heard it said that weightlifters are never at the height of their powers during competitions because of the psychological pressure bearing down. Non-professional actors, similarly, are more at ease in front of small, inconspicuous video cameras, with only a handful of technicians around, without the intimidating, crocodile-like clapperboard and all that other production paraphernalia. It shakes them up, which is why under such circumstances the camera can never capture a true reflection of someone's inner life. I planned a lengthy tracking shot for *Through the Olive Trees*, but the actors were uncomfortable with all those crew members around, so the cameraman put a long-distance lens on the camera and everyone moved fifty metres away. The further away we were, the better the performances became.

I have done my best to neutralise the presence of camera and crew, including searching for more discreet ways to start work than shouting "Action!" The appearance of digital technology and the possibilities these new cameras offer represent a profound shift in how we can make films, and to some extent my wish has come true. Lightweight digital cameras minimise the distance between actors and me. A sense of intimacy grows more speedily between us when we aren't surrounded by invasive equipment and crowds of people. This new technology allows for genuine freedom of action and has opened up possibilities that are suited to my style of working. For years I looked at the video camera as something only to take notes with, but when I began using it more seriously I came to understand the possibilities,

especially that I could do finally justice to reality. It seems I wasted years shooting on 35mm. There is a prayer that asks the Almighty to show things as they really are. And God created the digital camera.

❀ ❀ ❀

The video camera brings us back to the origins of cinema because of the freedom it offers. We can go into the streets with virtually no resources – only a single piece of equipment and an actor – and make a film. Leave the big productions to the big producers, while you busy yourself with inexpensive and more intimate projects. We live in a world where overpowering media systems shape our tastes and preferences, but this week I want you to work on expressing yourself through the simplest of means, using structures as far from those of capital and the mainstream as possible.

❀ ❀ ❀

A few years ago I went out with a friend to take photos. His camera was digital, mine film. I spent much time looking and watching. I would raise the camera to my eye, standing and moving from left to right, adjusting the focus, then decide against pulling the trigger. By the end of our trip I had taken nine photos, while my friend had nearly two hundred. I got two for the album, he didn't get a single one. The danger of digital is that a good photograph is more likely to be accidental. If you had to pay for every image you collected, there would be better films out there.

❀ ❀ ❀

When using digital technology, once you have made that choice – and made it for good reason – don't compare the quality of the image with anything else. Appreciate it for what it is. The difference between 35mm and digital is the difference between oil and watercolour. One isn't better than the other. Each has its own "rules." You can do different things with each. With the films you will be making this week, think digitally from the moment you conceive your idea. Create something that could be made only on video with a small, intimate camera. *Ten* is very much the film it is because it was made entirely in a car with two digital cameras. Making it on 35mm would have been like asking a wrestler to sprint a one hundred-metre dash. If I can make a film on 35mm, if the story can sustain it, if I feel the actors can handle it, I will use 35mm. For this workshop, our tools are digital. As they say in Persian, "If you reach out and can't touch the lady of the house, go for the servant instead." The camera is a faithful and fair observer of the joys and miseries of those who find themselves in front of it. For the next few days, let's bear witness with these digital machines.

❀ ❀ ❀

My films have dedicated audiences, people estranged from the world of commercial cinema. Too many films leave audiences unfulfilled, which means there is an opportunity for other kinds of cinema to win them over. Traditional Hollywood product is moving in a direction different from the one that cinema is best equipped for. The well-known secret behind the success of American film around the world is that much of it deliberately sets out to scare or amuse or reduce audiences to tears or laughter. With its locked in cause and effect it lacks all subtleties and uncertainties. What this sort of filmmaking generally doesn't do is ask an audience to think. In the long run, the presence of American cinema across the globe might be more influential than its military might.

❀ ❀ ❀

Every time I gain a member of the audience, I lose one too. I accept that for as long as I continue working, the size of my audiences will be relatively small. My films aren't watched by even the tiniest percentage of viewers in Iran. Distributors have no faith in them and never invest anything in ensuring they are seen, which makes for a self-fulfilling prophecy. I work independently, always following amy own path. I have never had to worry about attracting viewers because my films cost so little to make. If a film of mine doesn't make a fortune at the box office, it isn't as if I won't ever be able to make another. Producing ten seconds of *Star Wars* cost as much as one of my entire films. Money has never influenced the realisation of my ideas.

The important thing is having the courage to experiment and take risks without being intimidated by the fact that only six people might see the result. Do your work with no expectations beyond personal satisfaction. A friend told me that while others cultivate hectares of land, I grow vegetables in a flowerpot. When it comes to filmmaking, a lack of freedom often increases in direct proportion to available finances. Money becomes a burden.

❀ ❀ ❀

Audiences avoid films in direct proportion to their originality.

❀ ❀ ❀

Having an eye on Hollywood keeps me oriented. I ask myself, after those kinds of experiences as a viewer: what is the return on time spent?

❀ ❀ ❀

Having a camera in hand is an invitation to stop and stare, to concentrate on what surrounds us. The camera pushes me to pay attention.

❀ ❀ ❀

As audiences, we are in need of serenity, a respite, those moments when we can breathe deeply. Things need to slow down. The bombastic film – made by technicians and bureaucrats, not storytellers – will one day self-destruct. As soon as a film tries to make an impact on me, I back away.

❀ ❀ ❀

An artist's raw material comes from what he finds around him. For me, human beings – individuals – are the most important elements in a film. As filmmakers, you have more responsibility to them than you do to all that equipment within arm's reach.

❀ ❀ ❀

To create work that everyone around the world will understand, root yourself deep in your culture. Learn about it from top to bottom. Get to know the places, ideas and people, their loves and concerns. Some filmmakers want to travel the world and acquire knowledge, but all the knowledge in the world can be found within your own community. Familiarise yourself with everything around you, and your work will be universal. As Sohrab wrote, "No matter where I am, the sky is mine." There is poetry to be found in the everyday. Just open your eyes. Everyone thinks they are different from everyone else, that uniqueness beckons, but this is precisely what we all have in common. If something interests me and I decide to put it on film, there is a chance someone else will find it consequential. The storyteller drinks from a shared reservoir.

Rather than emphasise differences between people, I look for similarities and universalities, for commonplace experiences. Some people lead exceptional lives, different from our own, and certain filmmakers are forever in search of those characters. I go in the opposite direction. I look for ordinary lives during exceptional moments.

Political truths can be found in films that aren't explicitly political, that don't claim to be political. Poetic films dealing with human problems can be political. They just don't point an accusing finger.

I am Iranian. I have lived my entire life in Iran. I am influenced by everything going on around me at home and it's the Iranian government that issues me a passport. But I don't want my work to have an Iranian passport. At home they accuse me of making films for foreign festivals. But I make them for human beings.

If you X-rayed someone you wouldn't be able to tell what his race or creed is. The populations of every nation in the world – despite differences of appearance and religion and language and way of life – have much in common. Our mental frameworks are identical. Our blood circulates the same way. Our nervous system

and eyes are alike. We laugh and cry at the same time, we bear the same pain. My toothache is no different from an American's or a Frenchman's. We experience the same emotions, the same pangs of love. Human suffering is shared by everyone, and the sought-after ideal of a world with neither oppressors nor oppressed is ubiquitous. When we look out the window or walk in nature, the protective sky above and benign silences are the same everywhere. Move beyond political or cultural differences, and tragedy has the same meaning for everyone. The characters in many of my films speak Persian, but they have no specific nationality, which means every member of the audience can relate.

I have never encountered a particular kind of viewer that universally appreciates – or dislikes – my work. My films are comprehensible to all. Enduring cinema is about the similarities between us, no matter where we live and under what regime. A good film has no precise nationality. What's unfortunate is that the citizens of every country are represented by their government. A few years ago a team of American wrestlers visited Iran for a tournament and were amazed by the welcome they received. The merchants in the bazaars wouldn't accept their money for goods, and even wanted to give them presents. When the Iranians lost a match, they applauded the American wrestlers. The surprised Americans were so touched that they paraded around the stadium with an Iranian flag. Like sport, cinema helps reveal the truth beyond headlines. Governments construct borders, artists eliminate them.

Cinema has never been the best place for propagating messages. It doesn't have the power to effect radical change in society. Filmmakers are like children with their toys. They can play for hours at reinventing the world, but there comes a moment when the adults walk in and tell them it's time to wash their hands and get ready for dinner. I don't want to talk politics or political cinema with you, but let me say that though some people think filmmakers should seek to facilitate change, it seems to me that a truly influential film is one which reveals things that might previously have been obscure. If I can't alter someone's fate with a ninety-minute story, perhaps that person will at least think about something new after seeing one of my films, or experience unfamiliar feelings when reading a poem I wrote. Is a piece of wood pushed into the ground when a butterfly lands on it? Everything, regardless of size, has the potential to create an effect.

With the emergence of Iranian cinema on the international stage came a newfound awareness for many people. An unexpected but intriguing image of the country clicked into focus. The West discovered a different way of making films and more Iranian films than ever before were released in New York, London and Paris. This exposure and acclaim boosted our self-confidence and allowed for something of a loosening of censorship at home. Iranian cinema has always been more energetic than the government is in trying to keep it hidden. Art flourishes during times of trouble. It's a sort of defence mechanism. Cinema has a life of its own. It can be controlled to some degree, but never completely extinguished.

❀ ❀ ❀

Art isn't about forcing ideas on people. It's about drawing ideas from them. The poem will always vanquish the soapbox slogan.

❀ ❀ ❀

The newspaper journalist assembles facts until midnight, then writes an article which is on my desk the following morning. His work – often sensational and superficial – is full of raw and undigested facts, and inevitably has an expiration date. The artist's interests, on the other hand, are universal and timeless. He looks beyond the humdrum and ephemeral, perhaps processing and refining those facts for years before doing anything with them. Ultimately, he makes everything meaningful. Good poetry is consequential, regardless of time and place. Its power never diminishes. *Bicycle Thieves*, De Sica's film from 1948, has a specificity – the landscape and politics of postwar Italy – but also a profound significance for us today, no matter who we are and where we live. It's a film relevant for everyone. De Sica and his screenwriter Cesare Zavattini were sensitive to the fact that societies at every corner of the planet, at every point in human history, share the same pleasures and antagonisms, joys and hardships. They studied the environment around them, then created a cinematic poem which will live for generations. As with all genuine poetic expression, *Bicycle Thieves* is timeless. A film powered by an ideology is one likely to fade when the plug is pulled on those political ideas and that era reaches its end, which history shows will always happen eventually.

Art and politics complement each other. When one no longer functions, the other takes over.

❖❖❖

Be receptive this week and you will likely not just learn something new, but also teach the person next to you.

❖❖❖

It can be invigorating to live within walls and work within restrictions. Such things can, oddly, be liberating, as we are forced to learn how to evade and elude. Barriers compel us to react against them and manoeuvre beyond, just as a flow of water changes direction when blocked. They help us define ourselves and our work, refine our powers of deception, disarm the means of control. An architect friend of mine told me that when duty-bound to adhere to rules for construction, as when designing a building for an irregularly shaped plot of land, his work is more innovative than if he had complete freedom. I remember writing class at school. When there were no limitations on our work, when there no rules we were obliged to creatively bend, few of us produced anything of interest. But once a restriction was imposed – having to write about something specific, or in a particular style – everybody came up with something worthwhile. The constraints of the many strict poetic forms that exist offer vibrant challenges, and the resulting verse often has flavours that the poet himself never knew he was capable of.

People, fictional or otherwise, who cross boundaries do the rest of us a service. They let everyone know that existing limits are too confining, that we need more space in which to move. Someone once told me that my films are full of people who explore the extremes of their obsessions and do whatever they can to bypass certain rules upon which society is constructed. I can't say I have ever been aware of this aspect of the stories I tell, though it doesn't entirely surprise me. Few laws are important enough to be universally respected. They are made to be broken, and I clearly have sympathy with people who want to overstep them, to move past a certain field of action, to sneak around the regulations and restraints that envelop us. What I like about rules is that they forever stimulate the imagination.

At a workshop in Turin, participants started making films the first day. They were determined but disjointed pieces of work. On day two, the group imposed a limitation on itself: the camera was not to leave the building. There was an immediate intensity in the air. Everyone looked at each other and their surroundings with fresh eyes. It was enough just to glance out the window to find something interesting, or observe what we were doing right there in the room, at that very moment. By day three there was a camera in every corner. The limitation we imposed on ourselves led to innovative thinking. The so-called rules of cinema are useful only insofar as they restrict and push us to explore in new directions. Consider this when you make your film: after knocking on a door, you have only ten words of dialogue before whoever answers slams it shut.

❁ ❁ ❁

We live within certain boundaries, but anyone who really wants to make a film will do so, no matter what restrictions exist, no matter how difficult the situation. This applies to filmmakers everywhere, not just in Iran. At home, we never discuss the laws that constrain us, the rules and regulations under which we live, probably because we know how to circumvent them. My work as a filmmaker has been shaped by the directions in which I haven't been able to move. The difficulties faced by filmmakers in Iran since the revolution have pushed cinema in directions different from the ones in which it operated before 1979. There was chaos during the early years of the revolution because no one even knew what the rules were. Today, I am all too aware of the limitations imposed by the regime and what I am not permitted to show.

The boundaries I function within provide a sort of freedom of action and energy, just as they do for everyone in Iran who manages to exist in spite of everything. To get past the censors, all you have to do is think hard about what it is you want to show, then devise a novel way of showing it. This isn't unlike women on the streets of Tehran who find a way of letting a lock of hair hang free. Something always spills out from their hijab, if only

43

three strands. Every filmmaker working in Iran has found his own way of expressing himself, regardless of having to work under the shadow of censorship. You could even argue that creativity blossoms in direct proportion to unfavourable circumstances, that one definition of an artist is someone able to convert constraints into something creative. As Hafez writes, "Only that which has ensnared us can set us free."

The requirement that onscreen women be veiled has impacted filmmaking in Iran because few women wear the hijab in private. Showing a woman sick at home with a fever but still covered up because of mandatory religious rules, for example, would be as absurd as giving someone an injection through a pair of trousers. There is a divide between reality and the fact that certain things are forbidden when it comes to cinema, which is why in my films I show women only in public, and often in cars, where they are obliged to be veiled.

❀ ❀ ❀

An interesting film contains things the censor isn't sure he should remove.

❀ ❀ ❀

The revolution didn't change what I did. I'm not one of those filmmakers who aligns his work to contemporary trends. You see the same ideas – the same concerns and beliefs – both before and after 1979 in the work of genuine Iranian filmmakers. The cinema I create is personal. There is a unity and consistency to it.

❀ ❀ ❀

Cars are like horses, only more patient. They allow me to make contact with people at the roadside. All I have to do is wind down the window and ask for directions. I enjoy driving, and if I weren't a filmmaker I might have become a truck driver. I often give rides to hitchhikers who end up telling me things they wouldn't dare mention to their wives. Buckling your seat belt can be like lying on a psychiatrist's couch. I like these kinds of fleeting encounters, the fact that after an hour-long conversation, my passenger and I might never see each other again. My interior life is more intense in a car than at home. In my living room, I rarely have time to stop moving, but as soon as I get into a car I am forced to be inert. A traffic jam provides time to think. There are no disturbances, no telephones, no unexpected visitors. There is a beautiful stillness.

A car offers a sense of security. It's the best place I know for looking and reflecting, for facilitating endless conversations and the ongoing inner dialogue I have with myself. A friend told me that she and her husband have their most important discussions while driving because there is nowhere for either to hide. I feel more at ease sitting next to someone, without the weight of a stare from across the table. When you sit with someone in a car, side by side, with a shared view of the world, you almost always feel comfortable whether or not you know that person. Silences in a car never seem to weigh heavily. No one expects you to reply instantly to questions asked in a car. There is time to contemplate before responding. This intimate space is a home, a shooting location and an office rolled into one. I can get work done while in the driver's seat, looking through the windshield, as it continuously broadcasts images. One minute the rolling countryside is in view, a few minutes later the lonely suburbs appear, and eventually the ominous city reveals itself. It's a permanent tracking shot, with mirrors, like little televisions, on either side.

Perhaps my affection for cars is actually a love of roads. The idea of the journey, moving from one point to the next, is important in Iranian culture. The road is an expression of man in search of provisions, of the soul never at rest, of never-ending exploration.

❖❖❖

I am able to say whether I like a film or not, but it's not easy for me to go deeper and explain the reasons.

❖❖❖

On the days you aren't making a film, you aren't a filmmaker.

❖❖❖

Travelling by car is different from travelling by aeroplane. There is always a destination in mind when boarding a plane, and of course one rarely travels alone through the air. Not so with a car, which allows me to escape everything – including other people – and explore outside the city, where the terrain brings with it the constant possibility of new paths and detours. My point of departure is usually Tehran. The end point is the wide open, as welcoming as anything I have ever experienced, a world of infinite unexpected and unknown destinations, an environment that asks nothing of me, yet offers everything. I venture forth without knowledge of where I might sleep, of what there might be to eat. I just move and look and explore, camera in hand. I leave my house having planned nothing, knowing it might be days before I return home, and hours later find a small village where I encounter a family I have never met and will almost certainly never see again. They take me in, feed me, offer a bed for the night, and in the morning, before breakfast with Mother and Father and three children, I open the window of my bedroom and see before me a valley, a series of majestic, snow-capped peaks in the distance, and a few feet from the house a single tree, everlasting, its branches spread wide, standing in the whiteness, all of which the night before had been enveloped in darkness. The delights of chance. The value of improvisation. Overwhelming joy.

My car has been loyal to me, as patient as a horse. I care for it as I would an animal.

There is no steeper learning curve than writing a scene, then filming that scene – again and again – so your work contains fewer and fewer errors. You bring an increasing level of skill to each version, and also to your next project. It's the evolution of technique.

By day's end, I want you all to have at least one idea for a film you are going to make this week. At a previous workshop one participant made three films in two days. He had commendable ideas and brought with him a competent level of craft. Although he hadn't really thought things through, what I appreciated about him was that he never announced, "I'm going outside to make three films." He just appeared one morning and screened them. He never complained about how he couldn't find a location or how one of his actors didn't show up or that he had absolutely no experience with the equipment he was using.

Over the years I have encountered participants at these meetings who are terrified about getting to work because they think that whatever they put their name to has to be a masterpiece. They should, as far as I can see, step back from this feeling and consider instead that making a series of self-contained sketches of average quality would be a useful exercise. Don't think you have to make films good enough to be screened at festivals. Focus your attention on producing a handful of small, truthful films of five minutes each rather than a single complex work. Everything is permitted, but short films – shot and edited the same day – are sufficient. I can't say that every film made during previous workshops was good, but it was important they were made. Perhaps each was a stepping-stone to a stronger idea and a better film. If you don't have the tools to make big films, make small ones instead. We are all waiting for that open-minded producer to come along and finance our prized project. Until then, continue experimenting.

For a short, you need only one idea. My film *The Chorus* is seven minutes long and based on the simple concept that a man can't hear what is going on unless he is wearing a hearing aid. Don't complicate things. Don't waste a second. Cut to the chase. Sitting here, surrounded by colleagues, you shouldn't take five minutes to explain a five-minute film. Consider our work here together as merely warming-up exercises. Search your mind to see what memories suggest themselves, then come back tomorrow with your ideas. What rises to the surface might not be too weighty, but we have to start somewhere. There is nothing wrong with walking out of this room right now with a camera but without a complete idea. An exercise is like a piece of paper. You can work on it and learn from it, then throw it away and move on. Answers are useful only in that they lead to new questions. Cinema is in a state of permanent evolution. It will forever be a quest, a journey. Every film is a stage on the road.

I have been thinking about what idea might connect your films and whether there should be limitations imposed on your work here this week. In one previous workshop every participant made films involving a taxi, in another it was a cell phone, and in a third every film was inspired by Italian screenwriter Cesare

Zavattini, who believed that all we need do is look at the world around us for inspiration. For Zavattini, anyone can be the subject of a story. The people down there in the street are all we need for one hundred films. Workshop participants went outside and encountered complete strangers, the idea being that if you set up your camera in the middle of a crowd, the first person who walks past could be the perfect subject for a film. At a workshop in Tehran not long ago, we had only a single camera, angled on a passageway. Everyone took turns using it, stopping the first person who happened to walk by, which meant that everyone on screen came directly from real life. I could see participants exercising every ounce of their creativity to transform the circumstances that destiny had selected for them into intriguing and watchable films. It reminds me of prisoners, locked away, using plastic knives and dough to make sculptures, but who always succeed in creating something worthwhile.

As for self-imposed limitations this week, I have always thought an elevator would be a good location for a film. There is great potential for both drama and poetry when it comes to stories set in and around elevators. Within this enclosed room there is limited space, and presumably a film set in an elevator has to be of limited duration. Elevators make noise, some have interesting lighting, a few are ornate pieces of machinery, often there is music playing, and these days they have screens displaying information, news and advertisements. There are many different kinds: public or private, for passengers or heavy goods, clean or dirty, mirrors on every wall, or none at all. Some have doors that open – to everyone's surprise – on both sides. Some are so small that three people can barely squeeze in, others are big enough to carry cars up and down buildings. Older elevators need someone to operate them, perhaps a distinguished, elderly gentleman who has spent his life travelling to and fro, pushing buttons and pulling levers. Some trundle through decrepit buildings of only three or four floors, others fly at astonishing speed up and down modern metal skyscrapers of one hundred storeys. Some are high-tech and completely silent, some make much noise. People are constantly getting on and off, which is a good way of introducing and ejecting characters. Personally, I feel naked and exposed whenever I am in an elevator, forced to stand beside people I don't know. How best to break the awkward silence? Elevators are inevitably what we encounter en route to and from places and people, which gives them a metaphoric quality. We could even make an action film in an elevator by introducing an assassin on the ground floor and a hero on the top. Most of you have probably already been inside an elevator today. They are environments we all immediately understand, so start considering the circumstances that might lead you to make use of these machines, and a great many stories and characters will doubtless reveal themselves.

Picture a young couple. He proposes to her and asks that she answer by the time they reach the top, so she presses all the buttons to give herself as much time as possible. The movement of the doors opening and closing can show the passage of time and elegantly build in a sense of suspense. How long will this trip take? Will she answer in time? Will it be the answer he is expecting? Another scenario: picture a two-year-old in a lift. The doors open and he has become a ten-year-old. As the elevator moves up the building, he gets older, until, by the top floor, he is a stoop-shouldered old man. And, of course, travelling in an elevator means being in close quarters with other people, something that requires a certain etiquette, which might serve as a narrative device. An elevator could clearly be the setting for a number of sketches and small dramas. The possibilities are endless. It's a magic box for stories, so start thinking about creating stories that are connected to elevators. If you don't like that particular restriction, think of a different location or a visual theme we can all shape our ideas around. But do it quickly. This is a workshop, so let's do some work. Don't squander your time here. The only wrongdoing is inactivity. Just get going and don't ask too many questions. The work will guide you. Saadi tells us it's better to walk in the desert aimlessly than to sit idly. Rumi writes that to work hard with no outcome is preferable to being asleep.

"What's interesting," says Elisa, *"is that there are clear similarities between cars and elevators."*

I had never thought of that. Yes, an elevator is a vertical car.

"I have read so many stories by students set in elevators," says Benjamin, a teacher. *"It's a convenient metaphor, this idea of a journey, with the opening of a door and the traveller stepping out into an adventure. But most of the time it doesn't work."* Similar concerns are voiced by other participants. Aren't elevators too confining? Limitations are useful, but having to set every film in the same place seems too much of an impediment. The insistence on a physical location seems problematic when compared to thematic

or conceptual circumscriptions. "A theme can always be interpreted to fit the stories we all want to tell," says Julietta, "but having to film in a particular place locks us down too much."

I disagree. I already can't stop thinking of stories set in elevators. Someone wants to get to the tenth floor. He pushes the button and nothing happens, so he walks all the way up only to discover a young couple has held open the doors and are using it as a private room for themselves. Or we find a grandmother who travels, laden with gifts, from her faraway village to the city, where her son lives on the eighth floor of a tower block. She has never been in an elevator before. She pushes the button and the doors open, but she can't decide whether to get in. As she tentatively starts to step inside, the doors close on her. She finds this mildly insulting, even a little frightening, so she decides to walk up instead. On each floor, a little wearier from carrying her many gifts, she wonders if she should get into the elevator. On the fifth floor the elevator doors open momentarily and she sees a young couple inside. They are kissing. She walks up more flights of stairs. Eventually, exhausted, she has no choice but to push the button and wait. A man walks along the corridor and stands next to her. We see a sign behind the two of them that says "Eighth Floor." The woman hasn't noticed that she is actually where she wants to be. The elevator arrives and they both get in, but she pushes the wrong button and instead of going up, which is where she thinks she needs to go, the elevator takes her back down to the ground floor. She gets out with her packages and stares in confusion. It's a comedy. Remember that Laurel and Hardy short with the piano? Perhaps one or two of you will make films designed to coax a smile.

An interesting ending for each story, one that carries some dramatic momentum, is always good. We are working together, so if you have a good beginning for a story but no ending, or there is an image in your mind that intrigues but you don't know what to do with, perhaps we can work on it together. It's impossible that each of you don't have at least one elevator story in you. Here is another idea. A child enters an elevator carrying a telephone book. He puts it down and stands on it so he can reach the button for the third floor. He get out on the third floor and finds another telephone book just outside the door. He takes it, puts it down on the floor so he can reach the button for the fourth floor. And so on, until he gets to the top floor.

Sarah talks about being in the slow elevator of an office building and hearing people arguing on one of the floors below. "The doors opened and as soon as the people caught sight of me, they stopped arguing and stepped inside. Once we reached the ground floor and the doors opened, they walked out and immediately started arguing again."

This is good, certainly something we can work on. Why are people so polite in elevators?

"Proximity. You stand shoulder to shoulder with complete strangers," says Daniel.

"In Greece, Italy and other places people in elevators always talk to each other," says Elena. "It's only the English who are so reserved in front of strangers."

What about talking elevators, the ones that tell you which floor you're on? And these days some elevators have cameras in them. Rarely are you truly alone when travelling up and down a building. These are tiny spaces, but images from them are being broadcast to a crew of security guards in the basement, perhaps even further afield than that. How about a moment in an elevator that is over its weight limit because there are too many passengers? Someone counts the number of people and announces that three have to get out. But which three? A little old lady volunteers, but she weighs so little it makes no difference. I have no ending for this tale. You'll have to think of one yourself. And consider a film about an elevator that isn't set entirely in an elevator. What might that be? Think about a scenario involving a family living on the ground floor of a tall building and because of this isn't required to pay any money towards the maintenance of the elevator. But their young children end up using the elevator more than anyone else because they play in it all day long. Surely this situation will become a source of conflict between people in the building.

"I live on the tenth floor of a block," says Jessica. "I want to take two chairs and a slab of chocolate, and put them in one of the big elevators. Hopefully people will sit while they are riding up and down, and I can ask them questions."

What kind of questions?

"Perhaps something appropriate to each person, but I was also thinking of asking everyone, 'If this lift could take you anywhere in the world, where would you go?'"

Good. Asking people specific questions about themselves probably wouldn't be a good idea. But I wonder if by the time you explain what you are doing, there will be enough time to ask anything, much less hear what they say in response.

"I might put a small table inside and stick up a sign with the question written on it to save time. Once the doors open, people will work out what we're doing."

Pretend I have just got onto the lift. Ask me a question.

"If this lift could take you anywhere in the world, where would you go?"

Abbas pretends to think. He scratches his chin. He looks around. Twenty seconds pass.

It's my floor. I'm getting off here. You see? You have to be quick. People generally don't hang around in elevators, so write down some questions before you start, and beyond asking, "If this lift could take you anywhere," stay away from questions about elevators themselves. There are more interesting subjects.

"A person comes out of a noisy room," says Daniel. "We see he's a priest, apparently coming from a party. He's more than a little drunk. He gets into the lift and presses the button. His head slumps. We hear an argument from outside. The lift stops and a couple enter. They stop arguing because they want to be respectful in front of a priest. They think he's praying. Once they leave the elevator, their arguing immediately starts again."

This isn't a real priest, right? He has come from a fancy dress party?

"Yes. We make it clear he's not a real priest."

How?

"He's wearing a feather boa and lipstick, and smells of beer."

Will the audience be able to smell him?

Pause. "No."

Once we unpack this idea, it becomes more convoluted than you might at first think. As I understand it, your film functions only if the audience knows this isn't a real priest but the people inside the elevator think he is authentic and so act respectfully in front of him. That's the joke. How do we make both things absolutely clear? You might have other people coming out of the party before him, people dressed in other bizarre costumes, which makes it clear this is a party. But even so, why shouldn't a priest be wearing lipstick? Such things are no guarantee that he isn't a genuine man of God. It might be more interesting if from the start everyone – including the audience – thinks he is a priest, then

52

by the end of the film realises this man is no such thing. Always consider the flow of information to the audience, how best to feed certain things, little by little, and at the right time. Even if the goal is to share information, withholding can also be a useful tactic.

"Perhaps I'm alone in this," says Thomas, "but I feel it would be useful to spend some time watching your films and having you, Mr. Kiarostami, talk us through them. I know I would learn a great deal."

I'm not sure you would. There are basically two ways we can conduct these sessions. One is to talk about films, the other is to make them. We could sit here and deconstruct one of my films for hours at a time, even one of my shorts made more than forty years ago, because there will probably be twice as many interpretations as there are people in this room. But we should stop philosophising and get to work. For me to explain how I do things isn't going to be of much use to you unless what I say is somehow connected to practical work. At this early stage, the most important thing is that we put aside our trepidation of coming up with story after story. A group like this should be able to invent several workable ideas every hour. If my job is anything, it's to act as a catalyst. Put your minds together and throw everything out into the public forum. Today is our first day together, so we are exploring our own potential for the rest of our time here. You don't even know each other, but I assure you: we all are friends, a makeshift community of filmmakers moving forward as one. You probably have more in common than you think.

"Should we introduce ourselves to one another before we start work?" asks Joey.

Do that once you are actually making films together. Although at that point, of course, you won't need to introduce yourselves. Get on with things, side by side, and all will be revealed.

◈ ◈ ◈

Put away your computers this week. Turn off your phones. Resist the temptation to travel with them. The world becomes exactly the same, wherever you go, if you carry those machines. With them in your pocket the world is blocked, prevented from having an impact upon you. Leave all barriers at home.

◈ ◈ ◈

53

For tomorrow I want you all to think of a story. It should be comprised of images, those that have the potential to become an elevator film. We have to make these films cheaply and quickly, so think about stories that can take place in this city, here and now. This is, above all, an exercise to help you transfer memories and ideas into workable scenarios of films you can make today.

Let me tell you a story. It has nothing to do with elevators, but perhaps you will be able to see it in your mind – shot by shot – as I talk it through. Turn your mind into a camera, one able to float about in time and space. That's reason enough for me to tell it. The scene is São Paulo. I step out from my hotel into the city street. Five in the afternoon. Rush hour. The noise of heavy traffic and crowds of people. The air is hot and stuffy. A young boy walks past me. His face is dirty and sunburned, and he is wearing a black hat pulled down almost over his eyes. I look at his clothes and conclude that even though he walks with determination and confidence, the boy is homeless. A combination of my impressions – of his way of dressing, and how he moves through the hordes – prompt me to follow him. I watch as he stops at a litterbin and digs around inside. Not finding anything, he walks off quickly

to the next bin, in which he finds a half-eaten sandwich. It's covered in muck, so he puts it back. The boy moves from one bin to the next, looking through the contents of each with great care, picking things up, studying them, then putting them back. Eventually he notices me walking behind him, watching his every move. Our eyes meet. He jumps into the street as if to evade my gaze, running past moving traffic, and escapes to the other side from where he glances over – making it clear that he wants to be rid of me – before dashing off.

I lean against a lamppost, light a cigarette, and find myself standing next to a girl, perhaps thirteen years old, who is peering into a litterbin. She is wearing one-inch heels, two dirty T-shirts – one on top of the other – and has a green ribbon in her hair. I can't quite see her face. She walks from one bin to the next, looking in each, maintaining a distance, never digging with her hands. It's a different way of doing things than the boy. Where he was frantic, there is a certain dignity to this girl. She carries herself with pride and poise. When she finds the sandwich that the boy decided he didn't want, she picks it up, looks at it, places it back in the litterbin, takes a paper napkin from her pocket and wipes her hands. I decide to follow her. She walks over to a flowerbed next to a bus stop. I watch from a distance as she reaches down, picks up something from the flowerbed, and eats it. She does this several times. She doesn't chew, she just swallows these things while looking for more. A woman, who wears an overcoat buttoned from top to bottom, is standing, waiting for a bus, carrying shopping bags. She looks with curiosity – and a hint of disapproval – at the girl, but is clearly trying not to be noticed as she steals these glances. The woman is embarrassed when the girl eventually catches her staring. Indignant, with a skip in her step, the girl walks off. The woman steps over to the flowerbed to see what the girl was picking at. I also walk over, and our eyes catch for a second. A bus arrives and the woman hurries to board it. I stand there a few seconds more, looking down, inspecting the flowerbed, but can't work out what the girl was chewing on. There is nothing, or at least nothing I can imagine she would have been eating. I turn and see her walking down the street. I continue following and notice that the way she walks is different from everyone around her. She looks like a princess on an afternoon stroll through her vast, luscious gardens.

She stops at a litterbin in front of a fast food restaurant. By now, I'm convinced the girl is very hungry. There are small groups of people eating outside, on every corner of the street. "There are probably a dozen half-eaten hamburgers in that bin," I think to myself. "I'm sure she'll find something." But there appears to be nothing in there she feels is worth eating, so I walk into the restaurant, which is crowded. There are rows of people waiting to order food and use the toilet, people with either empty stomachs or full bladders. People queuing always look funny to me, perhaps because they are publicly declaring their private, inner needs in perfect unison. If I were to buy a hamburger it would take ten minutes and the girl would be long gone, so after standing for few seconds, I walk up to the counter, put some money down, and take the bag of food sitting there. No one seems to mind. Apparently they all think I'm not impolite so much as extremely hungry.

I walk outside and see that the girl is further down the street than I had anticipated, standing outside a jewellery store, looking intensely into the window. By this point, I haven't yet had a good look at her face, and really want to look into her eyes, so I walk past her and through the door of the jewellery store, which rings as I open it, alerting the owner to my presence. He welcomes me, but I turn and stare out through his shop window, ignoring his merchandise, and focus on the girl outside, her face partially lit by the dwindling light of the day. She is beautiful, made all the more so by Boccherini's Sonata for Harp and Flute, which plays inside the store. She eyes the jewels to her heart's content while I look to my heart's content at her, as the owner of the store is wondering who this man is, looking out the window and carrying a bag of smelly food. I stand there, having now seen this girl's face, seen into her luminous eyes, wondering if I could ever tire of such things, and realise she isn't staring covetously or with even a hint of envy. It also seems to me that she isn't the sort of person who would ever eat a cheap hamburger and French fries, however hungry she might be. She looks like the kind of woman who is hard to please.

She walks off and I leave the store – slightly embarrassed – without looking back at the owner. As I watch her ahead of me, I have an idea. The only thing to do is place the bag of food in a litterbin for her to find, as if by chance. I know what you're thinking. Who would throw an untouched hamburger into a bin unless it had gone bad? Having seen her clean her hands after touching the sandwich, it's obvious she's not going to eat anything she thinks is rotten. So I come up with a plan. I will take a bite from the hamburger, put the unfinished burger back in the bag, then place it into the litterbin which she is walking towards. As I take the bite, I realise I'm not in the least hungry and remember I have a dinner appointment in a couple of hours, so don't want to spoil my appetite. I spit the piece of hamburger out into my hand and place the bag into the bin before moving away from it, pretending to look into a shop window. She walks up to the litterbin, but before noticing the bag sees a Coca-Cola can standing on the ground next to it. She picks it up and gives it a shake. Apparently it's full because she starts drinking it down. It seems that she doesn't expect a litterbin to provide both food and drink because she walks on, ignoring the bag. I don't think she even sees it. I decide to pick it out of the bin and try again, so walk hurriedly up to the litterbin, grab the bag, walk past her and place it in the next bin, a few feet away. This time I feel fortunate that she still hasn't noticed me. Or, at least, I don't think she has noticed me.

From across the street I can hardly bear to look as she approaches the new litterbin. I see her peering into it, putting her hand inside, fumbling with something – does it really take that long to pick up a bag? – then walking away, inspecting her find. My view is obscured, so though I can see that she is carrying something, I'm not sure what it is. Eventually I see she has a magazine in her hand, but no bag. Another failure. But wait! After tearing a page from it she walks back to the bin. Perhaps now she will find the bag. But she throws the magazine from a distance, which lands directly in the bin, and walks away. I retrieve my bag again. By now I am fed up with this cat-and-mouse scenario. This girl is consistently failing to pay the proper attention to all the food lying in litterbins around the city. Surely I can't be the only person trying to feed the homeless by leaving hamburgers around town. Here I am, stuck with a bag of food. There she is, still with an empty stomach.

Again I walk past her and see she is absorbed in the page torn from the magazine, on which is a photo of a fashion model. I place the bag in yet another litterbin and wait. She walks by, still entranced by this magazine image, and puts the empty Coca-Cola can inside the bin before walking on. Perhaps she's not hungry after all. Perhaps it's just a figment of my imagination. Perhaps I have been wrong from the start. All she ever wanted was those morsels from the flowerbed to snack on and that photo to look at. I try to forget about the half-finished sandwich she picked up then threw away. Perhaps those dirty T-shirts are a fashion statement. No doubt her mother has told her countless times to make use of the washing machine at home and take some clean and ironed clothes from her closet. I feel a bit foolish, not least because by now my feet are aching and I am starting to get hungry myself. Then I notice she is looking into another bin with great intensity, like never before, and I kick myself for not having put the bag of food in that one. She walks off and I decide enough is enough. I will give the food to someone else, to the young man across the road sleeping in a huge cardboard box with the words "Handle With Care" printed on it. I couldn't say for sure whether he is hungry. Would a hungry man go to sleep so early in the evening?

But I can't do it. My heart is with the girl. I can't hand over her food to this man inside his box, no matter how needy he seems. By now the girl is standing over yet another litterbin, wiping clean an apple she has found. She holds this piece of fruit with two fingers and takes a small bite. For a moment it occurs to me that I could just go up to her and offer the bag, but that would be admitting defeat. It would be like cheating. I have to play according to the rules I have established in my head. She has to find this hamburger in a bin. Anything else would be a compromise, and I am in no mood to compromise. Yet again I place the bag into a bin, then watch as the girl throws her apple core into it, lights a cigarette, and walks away. Soon I can no longer see her in the dark of the evening. I stare into space down the street. A few minutes later, as I close the door of my hotel room behind me, I realise I still have that piece of hamburger in my hand.

Another story, this one much shorter. In 1970, at the age of thirty, I was travelling outside Iran for the first time. I was in Czechoslovakia and slept on trains because I didn't have much money. One night, a well-dressed gentleman carrying a briefcase and wearing a hat and overcoat got into the sleeper wagon. He opened the briefcase and took out a jacket, shirt and tie, then hung them up. He sat at the end of his bed and took off his shoes, socks and trousers. I was astonished at seeing his underwear pulled up over his huge belly. He didn't think anyone was watching him. Finally, he took off his hat. I remember how the nightlight reflected on his bald head. I stared as he slid into bed without rumpling the sheets. After only a few minutes, he got up and proceeded to put everything back on again, including his tie. As we arrived at the next station, he carefully placed his hat on his head, took hold of his bag, and stepped off the train. It had taken him ten minutes to remove all those articles of clothing and ten minutes to get dressed again. He was in bed for only five minutes. This is my train story, one of many I have from Czechoslovakia. I often replay this series of shots in my mind. It's the best film I never made. Doubtless all of you screen films continuously in the privacy of your head, each time refining and elaborating. Let's hope a few of them take place in elevators.

There might not be an elevator in this building, but there are probably a dozen within two hundred yards of where we are sitting, including all those nearby museums. They have beautiful interiors and are packed with people. For our purposes, there is no such thing as an impractical elevator. If you find one, you are sure to find no end of stories. In Turin, a workshop participant bought a bright red bra which he dropped onto the floor of an elevator in a hotel frequented by wealthy businessmen, then filmed the expressions on their faces. I hope one of you takes a camera and stakes out an elevator in an interesting public place, like a hotel or hospital. Be the first person to return with a film.

"*Do you have any advice for those of us who plan to shoot this evening?*"

Advice? Do a good job.

❁ ❁ ❁

Day two.

Don't be late again. We start at nine o'clock.

I hope you went to bed last night thinking about elevators. I know I did. If you have an idea you think is worthwhile, it doesn't matter if no one else likes it or has nothing to say in response. Just tell us. And be as concise as possible.

"*A friend told me he once moved apartments from the second to the tenth floor of the same building,*" says Adam. "*He put everything he owned in the elevator. His entire life travelled up eight floors.*"

This is a background to a film, not a story in itself. The key is to start thinking cinematically. Don't tell us what your stories are about or what your concept is. Just explain with minute precision what we see and hear. At all times be specific, and don't tell us anything before we need to know it. Your ideas will hopefully become clear once the story starts playing out in our minds as sounds and images, once we see your characters doing things and talking to each other. Taking your example as a starting point, how about this: a woman walks up to an elevator carrying a chair. Outside the elevator are some boxes. She puts the chair down and pushes the button. She waits. When the doors open she picks up the chair and goes inside, puts the chair down, then hurries out to grab the boxes. She isn't quick enough. The elevator doors close behind her, leaving her stranded on the landing, her chair inside. On another floor, a man is waiting for the elevator. It arrives. The doors open and reveal the two chairs sitting there. I don't know what happens next, but I like this idea. Maybe the neighbours are annoyed that the elevator is being used in this way, so they start taking the furniture that this woman is transporting around the building.

"*Is there an elevator in your hotel?*"

Yes, and last night I spent time exploring it. I travelled up and down for nearly an hour. I can't imagine what the hotel staff thought I was doing. At one point a man got on and immediately started fidgeting. It annoyed him that we stopped at several floors on the way up to his room, and I clearly heard him exclaim, under his breath, "It would have been faster to walk up!" Why did the elevator aggravate him so? What upset him even before he got onto the elevator? Why was he in such a hurry? Was he expecting to find something or someone in his room that he couldn't wait to see? Later, a different passenger started banging on the walls because he was so drunk. He fell against the buttons and pressed them all, which meant we went through a slow routine where the elevator stopped on every floor. Each time the doors opened, he looked out into the corridor and – without once looking me in the eye – asked me where we were. On one floor directly opposite the elevator is a green sofa. Next to it is a table on which is a vase of beautiful blue flowers. A grey-haired man was sitting there, alone, deep in silence, wearing a suit and red tie, staring out at the world.

"*I recognise people in the elevator where I work,*" says Nicole, "*but don't know them well enough to strike up a conversation. How about a film where an elevator breaks down and two people are stuck, but still they don't talk to each other, communicating instead only in body language and eye contact until help arrives. Maybe we sense a flirtatious moment between them, but a close-up of wedding rings on both their hands tells us all we need to know.*"

I like the authenticity and simplicity of this moment, and also because of the opportunity it offers you to play with images. Not a single word needs to be spoken. Perhaps by the time she decides to respond to his smile, he has noticed her ring and is already looking at his shoes.

"*Years ago I went to Berlin with a friend,*" says Boris. "*We arrived back at our hotel after a night out and got into the elevator, which was big enough for only four people. Suddenly six people walked into the lobby and squashed themselves into the elevator.*"

One immediate question. Where do we put the camera? These are images that need to be converted into pieces of cinema. Always think of the practicality of your ideas. If they remain here in this room and are never realised, they aren't much use to us.

"*Perhaps we can cheat and film it with the doors open,*" suggests Boris. "*Some of these people started bouncing up and down as a joke, and the elevator stopped between floors. It took half an hour before the fire brigade got us out. What was interesting is how the various characters changed in this short time. The happy drunks who had pushed into the elevator quickly became angry, while my friend and I – who were annoyed at first – resigned ourselves to the ridiculousness of the situation and stayed calm. People seem to reveal their true selves when under pressure.*"

This is an interesting idea, but you need to stop telling us what your films are about. At one workshop there was a participant who, when talking about his idea, started off by saying: "This is a story of a man unhappy at the world, who wants to take revenge on society. It's about powerlessness and decay." And so on. No one wants to be told what a story is about. We make up our own minds about that. If your story isn't understandable through what the audience sees and hears, then no amount of explaining – either here or to people after they have watched your film – is going to make a difference. Describe your ideas only in images and sounds. Think about what the audience needs to see, plan your shots accordingly, then precisely describe those images to us. When do we cut to the happy drunks? How long does it take before they start to act disruptively? Exactly how do you and your friend respond? Start thinking in these terms now and it will be easier – faster, in other words – when you stand there with your camera rolling. Be specific, to the point of letting us know how long each shot lasts.

"I was thinking about a broken-down, pitch-black elevator and two people talking about their fear of the dark," says Sarah. *"We hear what might be sounds and talking from other elevators in the building, but we aren't sure. Then the lights come up to reveal two people – both men or both women, it doesn't really matter – who are clearly quite different from each other. One, for example, is a punk rocker, the other wears a business suit. They don't say a word to one another once the lights are on, which means we never know who said what. I suppose the film is about not judging a book by its cover."*

I like this idea of a conversation between two people whose identities are unknown to each other, though this story could take place in any darkened room. Can you integrate into the story the fact that they are in an elevator? Perhaps you need to simplify things and remove the idea of sound effects from other elevators. It's enough that we don't know who is talking. Don't divide the audience's attention and your energies. Grab hold of one idea and stick with it. Don't move on until you have solved any problems. Sharpen your focus. Find solutions. Get it right.

"Is it a good idea to build a story from the starting point of a specific character?" asks Nicole.

Come up with one and we can work on it. I have occasionally met people so interesting that an entire film was constructed around them. Originally, Mania Akbari was going to have only a small role in a film I wanted to make. My idea was of a therapist whose office has been closed by the authorities because one of his female patients insists that he encouraged her – against her will – to separate from her husband. The next day he encounters a patient at the entrance to his office and, making excuses, tells him that a water leak has flooded the room where he holds his therapy sessions. The patient – by now extremely distraught – gets into the therapist's car and refuses to leave. In the meantime, a policeman arrives and orders the therapist to move his car, so the session takes place on the move. Mania was going to play one of the other patients, but her talents were soon revealed and I decided she should play the therapist instead. When it dawned on me that she doesn't look or sound like a therapist, I scrapped the whole idea. It also turns out, of course, that therapists don't say very much. They just listen, and I didn't want to make a film full of monologues. The subject of the conversations I planned eventually gravitated towards relationships between women. The result is *Ten*, where Mania drives around Tehran giving rides to various women she picks up, including a prostitute, a wife who has been abandoned by her husband, and an elderly woman on her way to mosque. Godard said that all you need to make a film is "a gun and a girl." For me it's "a girl without a gun," or perhaps "a girl in a car." Who else has an idea?

"An elevator is moving with only a woman inside," says Beatrice. *"Close-up on her face. Her expressions are changing."*

If it's a close-up, how do we know the elevator is moving? How do we know she's alone? How do we even know she's in an elevator? You understand why I am asking these questions? As you tell us your stories for the first time, describe only what we need to know. As we consider the images you give us, as we play out your film in our heads, if it's not clear to us that she is alone, then you need to re-think your shot list. Is it even relevant to the story that she's on her own? If not, why tell us? We need only the most basic facts about who is in the frame, what they are doing and saying. Once we have this information – as we bring to mind the pictures and sounds – if it's not immediately obvious to us what the story is, there is a problem.

"OK. A woman is in an elevator…"

Give us your shot list.

"Close-up on a woman's face. The noise of an elevator, maybe each floor being announced. As the elevator moves up, light from outside bleeds through the crack of the door onto her face."

Good.

"We see disbelief, then anger, then deep pain. Her eyes fill with tears. She fights them back with steely resolve. Her eyes tighten. Cut to the fourteenth floor where a young man is waiting for her."

How do we know he is waiting for her? What do we see him doing that makes it clear to us that this is what's going on? If we can't immediately tell that he's waiting for her by what he is doing or how you film him, don't tell us.

Beatrice pauses. "The doors open on the fourteenth floor and we see a young man. Their eyes meet. His are full of anticipation and longing. Hers are cold and questioning. The doors start to close. He grabs them. The two stare at each other. She removes his hand from the doors. The doors close. The elevator goes down. Her face shows heartbreak and loneliness. She flattens out non-existent creases from her clothes. She seems confident as she steps out from the elevator into the lobby and outside to the street."

Very good. If you can see the story in such detail, then you are at the point where you should film it. I'm glad you didn't explain what it all means. Once your work is done, once we are all sitting together and watching it, you won't be able to stop everyone from interpreting it, so there's no need for you to relate your own feelings about such things now. By the way, it isn't necessary to describe her face as full of heartbreak and loneliness, and her expressing such confidence. This is your need to explain things creeping in again. Cut an image of her face – even one still and expressionless – into the film at that moment of the story, preceded by all those other images, and the audience will likely feel those emotions and take note of her confidence whether you want it to or not. Let me ask you a question, which you don't have to answer: did something inspire this tale?

"A friend of mine saw someone crying in an elevator, but couldn't get closer to help because he is claustrophobic."

Interesting. These are the moments and glimpses of reality that can inspire entire stories. Go shoot it. I have an idea. Two people, A and B, enter a lift. Other people come in on another floor. Close-ups of the pockets on their jackets, then their hands by their sides. We see A's hand move to B's pocket and take his wallet. A puts the wallet into his own pocket. A few seconds later B's hand moves towards A's pocket and steals his own wallet back, placing it in his pocket. It could be amusing if done well.

"It might look like two friends just fooling around with each other," says Jessica. "It needs to be clear that they are thieves who don't know each other."

I don't think the audience will see them as friends. The easiest way to avoid confusion is to have them get on at different floors so they don't seem connected, and perhaps have them appear different from each other. The way someone is dressed can be a quick and efficient way of conveying character. Any more ideas?

"We're inside a lift," says Efrat. "It's empty. The doors open at the fifth floor. A clown walks in dressed in white and has a big smile painted on his face. He's had a long day and is exhausted. He pushes the ground floor button."

You know what I'm going to ask.

"How do we know he's had a long day?"

If all we can see is this smile, how do we know he's tired?

"Maybe a close-up on his eyes that he can't keep open?"

Perhaps. Or how about having him carry something that makes it clear that he is exhausted. Is there some prop or action you can give the actor to make this clear? Something you can put into his hands? A good filmmaker understands that internal conflicts are just as important as the external, physicalised struggles taking place. Knowing how to make these struggles visible is a valuable skill. In this case, how about a handful of deflated and pathetic-looking balloons? And perhaps his make-up is smudged.

"He pushes the button wearily or drinks from a cup of coffee," says Efrat. "Then he hears a couple arguing. They get in on the next floor, full of energy, shouting at each other. Perhaps the lift breaks down."

That's all you have?

"I like the imagery."

It's enough to start with. The contrast between the dreary clown and animated couple is engaging. Don't worry about not having an ending. Talk to your colleagues and work out what happens next. You have enough for the beginning of a film. Any other ideas?

"A young, newly married couple have low-paying jobs and are frightened by the city," says Sandy.

Is this about an elevator?

"Eventually, yes."

It seems like a long story.

"Not really. This is just backstory."

Then why tell it to us? If the backstory isn't obvious to us after your shot descriptions, it isn't important. Put it out of mind.

"It's just an idea at the moment, not a script."

We are already on the second day of a seven-day workshop. Can ideas be filmed? Possibly, but only if you turn them into characters, actions and objects that can be placed in front of a camera. Think before you speak. If you can't condense any backstory into images, those details are probably unimportant. Start thinking in images rather than ideas.

Beatrice puts her hand up. "A lady is terrified of elevators. Can I say that?"

How are you going to show it?

"She lives in a high-rise and is nervous."

Does she have medical records pinned to her jacket?

"She stands in the lobby of a building. Usually she asks the doorman to accompany her to the door of her apartment, but today he isn't there and she can't bring herself to get into the elevator on her own."

If there is no doorman, how are we meant to know there usually is a doorman? And how are we meant to know what she usually does? Film isn't the best medium with which to show something that isn't there.

"She calls her husband on a pay phone and asks him to come to her assistance, but he doesn't answer."

How do we know it's her husband? Why am I struggling to get through to you? Just tell us everything we see, nothing more. A character's intention is made clear only through their actions. It's all very clear to you, in your head, but to us it's a jumble. In my experience, someone unable to stand up and describe their story in as simple terms as possible is likely not to have the skill to turn that story into a film.

"OK, so it's not her husband. It's someone. Anyone. We don't know exactly who. But whoever she calls isn't at home, so she walks out into the street and asks for help. Everyone ignores her. She decides to go into the elevator anyway, but as soon as the doors close she panics and pushes the alarm button."

I like the images, and the emotions are real enough, but I think a story of a woman who has never been in a lift before, rather than someone who is frightened of them, is more interesting. Who has never been in an elevator? Where is this woman from? She lives in a building with an elevator and this is her first time using it?

"I have been thinking about a character-based film featuring a woman who has never seen a lift before," says Joseph. "She is terrified and feels intensely claustrophobic."

It's fine if this is just a sketch, a scene that lasts a couple of minutes featuring this woman, but if you want anything more than that, something actually has to happen to her. Are there any other characters you can introduce? Do you know anyone who could play the part convincingly?

"I think I do know someone who looks vulnerable enough," says Joseph.

How do you specifically show her nervousness?

"I was thinking about her having a telephone number written on her hand, or on a chain around her wrist with her name on it. This would suggest that she has Alzheimer's. It's more bewilderment than nervousness."

It's a good visual idea. Work on it today and film it tomorrow.

"What I have is just a visual joke," says Naomi. "We see a hotel elevator, filmed at floor level. A red carpet. Shiny shoes. Cut to a man wearing a dressing gown strolling down the hallway and into the elevator. Shot at floor level again. Amid this sea of black leather we see his slippers. I don't have an ending."

It's enough for a two-minute film. This is the sort of thing that is probably going on at this very moment in my hotel. Last night I saw a man and woman in the elevator. They had just got out of the swimming pool and were wrapped in towels, surrounded on all sides by men in suits, carrying briefcases. That elevator seems to be a never-ending source of stories.

Susanna puts up her hand. "A woman, late thirties, stands in a hallway, waiting for an elevator. She pushes the button and takes a sandwich from her bag. The lift arrives. She gets in and starts eating. The elevator goes up a couple of floors and stops. The *doors open. Just before they close, a man gets on. He pulls out a handkerchief and wipes his forehead. He is tall, clean-shaven and wearing a suit. The woman finds him attractive."*

How do we know she likes him?

"This is the idea of the film. Before he got on the lift, she was eating the sandwich messily, without caring how she looked. Once he is standing next to her, the woman quickly and furtively tries to clean herself up because she wants to look good for him. She reaches into her pocket for a tissue but can't find one."

If she doesn't find a tissue, how do we know she's looking for one?

"I think it will be clear enough that she's digging around for something she can use to wipe her mouth," says Susanna.

"What if we see her look into the mirror at the back of the lift and notice egg salad around her mouth," suggests Boris.

Good.

"She can't find a tissue," continues Susanna, "so the man takes another handkerchief from his pocket and gives it to her. He smiles. She is embarrassed, but happy they have made contact. She smiles. The lift stops, he walks out. 'What about your handkerchief?' she says. 'Don't worry,' he says. 'I know which floor you live on.'"

It's a good idea, about how men and women react to each other, especially when in such close proximity. I also like the fact that you use the lift as an integral part of the story, and that the story is conveyed almost entirely in images. There is a lot of information you can give the audience through body language, the way she handles the sandwich and handkerchief, and herself more generally. She might try to fix her hair in the mirror or brush crumbs from her face. But why does the man mop his brow with a handkerchief? Is that necessary? Better for him to save his handkerchief for the woman's egg salad. Would he really have two handkerchiefs in his pocket? And how does he know which floor the woman lives on? He gets on the lift after her and gets off before her. Better to have her get off the lift first and hand him the handkerchief as she leaves. He refuses it, then comes out with that line.

"I'm wondering if you would like to see some of us make silent films this week," asks Cyrus.

Not necessarily. Human beings and the way they talk will always be a vital element of cinema. How can we expect to fully understand a character if we eliminate all dialogue from a film?

Words are profoundly suggestive. Even the name of someone you have never met has the power to create an immediate emotional association in your mind and conjure up an image. Without facial expressions, cinema would be incapable of depicting the solitude and beauty of man, but the same could be said about the intonation of someone's voice, which reveals as much about them as their eyes. When you telephone someone, you can sense their true intentions and what mood they are in just from the way they say hello. Something so revealing should be exploited as an integral component of filmmaking. There must be good reason to omit sound from a film entirely. If you chose to do so, give some clue in the image as to why that decision was made. Best to include a few sound effects, because if you produce a completely silent film and someone buys a DVD of it, they are likely to think something is wrong and ask for their money back.

Everything should fade away in the interests of the film as a whole. Just as a good musical score isn't necessarily one that people whistle for days afterwards, a powerful image doesn't have to be a beautiful and intricately constructed one that stands out from everything around it. A powerful image might be a simple snapshot of a landscape or a passing moment of emotion expressed by an actor, even a rapid glance of the eye.

When I first started out, I wanted to demonstrate my technical skills as a filmmaker, mainly because people were always telling me I was so lacking in such things. I ended up including fancy hand-held camera movement in my first film. The shots were interesting enough but my attempts at technical virtuosity clearly got in the way of the story. There must always be a good reason to move the camera. I can't deny that my camera set-ups are usually quite simple, that I prefer to strip the crew and equipment down to a minimum. In fact, for years cameramen didn't want to work with me because they considered my filmmaking to be so unsophisticated. But to focus on anything other than the story is to short-change the audience. If there is anything lasting in your film – if there is poetry – it will reveal itself through the characters, their interactions, and the landscapes they explore together, not a flamboyant camera technique.

Create a story in your mind before you film it. Edit your film in your mind before you edit it on your computer. Don't just hope for the best.

❀❀❀

Painters and poets have been representing things abstractly for thousands of years. Omit the colour green from a leaf and we see that leaf in a different way. It brings to mind something other than a leaf. We understand things not because of our immediate reality, but through associations.

❀❀❀

Does anyone mind if we finish early today? I would very much like to take a walk around the neighbourhood. Feel free to join me.

❀❀❀

Day three.

Several workshop participants are outside filming. Kiarostami sits with a small group. "Are there any tricks to maintaining good working relationships with non-professional actors before and during filming?" asks Naomi.

I am not a good enough writer to imagine what a teacher from the provinces might say or how he would react in certain situations. Who can write dialogue for an illiterate worker, a taxi driver or a religious old woman better than an illiterate worker, a taxi driver or a religious old woman? Often, when I have an idea I think is worth exploring, I go in search of real people who can embody the fictional characters of this unfinished story and thereby stimulate my imagination. When I find someone I feel might work as a character in a film, I spend time with him in his environment and, if possible, at the locations where I want to shoot. I learn about who he is, then use that information to shape my ideas. I don't interfere too much in what he does. I give a minimum of information, leaving enough space for him to express himself, and let him be. Using non-professional actors means certain rules apply. Because they essentially play themselves, you have to accept that they don't make mistakes and can never be

71

wrong. A lay performer swiftly lets it be known just how far his performance can be determined by the director. Permit a level of freedom in such situations. Don't try to control everything.

I always have something in mind when I embark upon projects of this kind, even if my vision is never set in stone. People with fixed ideas about who they want to fall in love with are likely to spend their lives alone. It's best to keep invented characters approximate and slightly out of focus, so that when I encounter someone in real life, my ideas are sufficiently malleable to allow me to perceive them as the person in my mind. Don't squeeze someone real into the rigid conception of a fictional character. Better to do things the other way round. Rather than pull someone closer to my constructed image – hoping that reality will conform – I adjust and shift myself towards the real person, to the situation as it plays out in front of me. My original idea is like a piece of cloth trimmed according to the needs of the actor who has to wear it. If the jacket is too big, the tailor doesn't say, "Go home, shorten your arms and come back in the morning. Then the jacket will fit you." What he does is adjust the sleeves.

Having said that, though I don't tell non-professionals exactly what their character says or does, I do try to subtly impose my thoughts, which means that in some measure my ideas become infused with the actor's. I explain the scene I have in mind, offering details about the narrative and general feeling and direction in which I would like to move. By doing so, I gently draw the actor towards the loose ideas I have of the character he is playing. At the same time, I know the actor will bring much of himself to the role. Most people play themselves very convincingly, which is why I don't interfere when, for example, it comes to how they dress. I let them correct me about such things. Lay actors are the best costume designers and make-up artists for themselves because no one knows better than they do what their character should wear. When someone stands in front of the mirror, matching her inner feelings with her outer look is more important than matching the colour of her shoes with the bag she carries. In real life we often come to understand someone instantly because of outward aspect and demeanour, even before a word has been uttered.

Working in this delicate way, after a period of time – sometimes months – it becomes hazy which ideas come from my imagination and which from the realities of the people playing the characters. It's about creating the right balance between the instructions I give non-professional actors and the information they give me, about helping develop their character and allowing them to make certain discoveries, about making sure they feel comfortable doing more or less what I want without my having to give direct instruction. Sometimes I don't know whether I am telling them what to say or they are writing their own script. We learn from each other.

※ ※ ※

Laziness is a sin.

※ ※ ※

You can't expect to create cinema without some sort of story. Even a still photograph has a narrative. But mystery is vital. The unresolved and mythic – not the resolved and rational – are what maintain our interest, and do so long after we have finished staring at a painting or reading a poem or watching a film.

※ ※ ※

Being clear and comprehensible requires hard work. Sometimes the most elementary stories are those that need the most thought. Don't confuse simplicity with ease of construction. The trick, in fact, is to make something complex look straightforward.

※ ※ ※

Accept that there is nothing new under the sun. Everything has been done already. But every creative artist brings a fresh outlook.

※ ※ ※

Remove everything unnecessary. Resist the onslaught of secondary ideas that come with your primary one. Don't adulterate. The most effective way of refining your work is to keep it short and simple. "I didn't really do anything," explained Michelangelo when asked how he created David. "The statue already existed in the block of stone. All I did was remove everything unnecessary." Rumi advises us not to talk too much, to use the fewest words possible. Consider this idea when telling your stories, when making films, when selecting images, when living life.

The language I use is aimed at imparting information as efficiently as possible. Sometimes I have ideas I am unable to express in words, so I don't write them down. A different form of expression is needed.

❁❁❁

Each shot should relate to every other shot.

❁❁❁

Concentrate! Don't be so impatient.

❁❁❁

Self-expression should almost always be kept private.

❁❁❁

Asking a non-professional actor to learn dialogue word-for-word rarely works. Usually, once we talk about the character he is playing, once I explain the scene, he ends up expressing himself far beyond what I could ever have imagined. I direct, as it were, indirectly, with a light touch. Give a performer space and it quickly becomes obvious he is the best person to tell you everything important – all those sensitive details – about his character. He knows how best to define that invented person and strip him of artificiality. Without specific lines to learn, he becomes tremendously resourceful, offering ideas and creating his own dialogue. By doing so, he puts more of himself into the role and moves things along in a lively direction. It can be a wonderfully surprising and invigorating experience for me.

The grandfather in *Where is the Friend's House?* has a monologue about how children should best be raised. He talks wonderfully about how, when he was a child, his father gave him a penny every week and a beating every fortnight. "Sometimes he forgot the penny," he says, "but he never forgot the beating." The grandfather commiserates about how children these days are so unruly, lacking in discipline, disrespectful of their elders. I spent time chatting with the old man, sitting beside him, drinking tea, before he knew I was making a film. I told him what I felt about youngsters today, agreeing with him that they are shamefully disobedient of their fathers. I went on and on until finally I explained what we were doing in the village, adding, "I would like to include this idea in the film, but no one will listen to me. Someone else is needed to explain such things, someone with a certain gravitas. I was going to ask my own father to appear in the scene, but he isn't feeling well. You remind me of him, and I wonder if you would consider playing the part. When it comes to expressing ideas like these, only an older man can be heard. If you were to talk about this business, people would surely listen." I planted certain seeds in his mind, then made it clear that he was the only person who could cultivate them. I manipulated him by giving him a big dose of self-confidence, so when we filmed the scene the old man felt no pressure and played it with absolute conviction and believability.

Sometimes I talk endlessly with an actor about a particular idea, hoping to convince him that the original thought was his in the first place. Hossein Rezai, who plays Hossein in *Through the Olive Trees*, helped shape and refine his character, always bringing me back to reality by questioning the truthfulness of certain lines of dialogue. Hossein and I met regularly for months before filming started. When I said something to him, and the look on his face told me I must be off-track, I would rethink my approach. Anything that seemed artificial and false was discarded. At one of our meetings, in the middle of the conversation, I said, "It would be a good thing if the rich could marry the poor. Then everyone would be able to have their own house. There is no point in having two houses. You can't put your head in one and your feet in the other." Later, when we met with the cameraman, I turned to Hossein and said, "Tell him what you told me about people having two houses." He looked at me, wondering for a moment if it was him or me who had originally talked about this. Eventually he repeated the idea to the cameraman, and I told him those weren't the exact words he had used before, or perhaps I added another line, pretending that he had been the one who originally said it. Every time I met with Hossein I asked him to repeat what he had said. Little by little, he absorbed the lines, which were now embedded in his memory. After about a month he came to believe they were all his own. Like hair implants, I could do only one or two clumps at a time.

That line about two houses is in *Through the Olive Trees*, when Hossein is in the car talking with the character of the film director, played by Mohammad-Ali Keshavarz, a professional actor. On the morning of the shoot, I walked with Hossein through the forest. "Do you remember, all those months ago," I asked him, "you pointed out to me that…?" I reminded him what he had said and suggested he tell Mr. Keshavarz about it. Hossein, who spoke the lines quite naturally and truthfully, had made them his own. Because of the way we worked together, they really did belong to him. Forcing a script on him and telling him what to say wouldn't have worked. I was the one sitting next to him in the car at the time, operating the camera and talking to him. When he said, "It's not possible to put your head in one house and your feet in another," it was me – not Mr. Keshavarz – who replied with the line, "But you can rent out one house and live in the other." The extraordinary look he gives is one of my favourite moments in the film. He forgot about the camera and reacted without thinking. Later on, I filmed the reverse angles on Mr. Keshavarz and cut the sequence together. Look at the scene again. Apart from the opening seconds, you never see the two of them together in the same shot.

Solid storytelling will always overpower the pictorial. But while the true foundation of a film might be the expression of ideas, know that a beautiful image – used in an appropriate way – can be a worthy one. There is value in such things.

Cinema, like poetry, is about rhythm.

I couldn't tell you what "great art" is. I know only of poems and films, of paintings and literature, that have taught me things and pointed me in new directions. And that contain beauty.

I enjoy working with actors who have no preconceptions. Professional actors are rarely so unadulterated, especially if they have had uneasy experiences with other directors, which means that part of my job can include the undoing of past associations and negative memories. They have worked on their technique for years and always ask so many questions. Every detail about their character is important to them, which means I am sometimes required to communicate using technical language. Non-professionals, however, rely solely on instinct and are forever forcing me to adjust my preconceptions. The two approaches rub off on each other, and the end result – a mix of professionals and non-professionals in the same scene – can be arresting. I cast William Shimell, an opera singer, in *Certified Copy* because I thought it might somehow influence Juliette Binoche's performance. I hoped he might challenge her in interesting ways, but William turned in a more polished performance than I expected. Perhaps the influence went the other way. Perhaps it was Juliette's professionalism that stirred William to act as he did.

Both expert and lay actors, in an ideal world, give believable performances, but they approach their tasks in completely different ways. It's best that an actor knows either absolutely everything about his craft and is at all times striving to improve his technique, or knows nothing at all. Anything in between these two extremes is problematic. The moment a professional steps onto the film set, he immediately becomes someone else. His job is to no longer be himself. The further he moves away from his true self, the closer he becomes the character he is playing. He knows everything there is to know about the technical apparatus and intricate procedures that surround him when he stands in front of the camera, but has trained himself to ignore it all. The professional has to be so expert at his job that everything he says and does is truthful. He has to create that believability through craft and conscious technique. The non–professional, on the other hand, approaches his work in an unconscious way. By being himself, by bringing nothing other than his true self to the set, he does what is required.

In *Through the Olive Trees*, whenever Hossein was in front of the camera, Mohammad-Ali Keshavarz was behind it, carefully studying his non-acting. It was almost as if he were asking himself, "How does this young man, who knows nothing about acting, manage to act so well?" The answer is that most non-professionals aren't acting when in front of the camera. They are being themselves. If you expect anything more from them than that, you will likely run into trouble. I avoid bringing notes or scripts with me to the set because they make lay performers uncomfortable. Two things can happen when non-professional actors look at the pages in my hand. Either they insist that memorising all those lines is impossible for them, or attempt to memorise the lines before acting them out. By doing so, the non-professional becomes a professional, and usually a bad one. Non-professionals should stay non-professional.

⚛ ⚛ ⚛

Good professional actors feign what competent lay actors do naturally, which is hold themselves in front of the camera precisely as they do in real life. I came to realise the truth of this insight as early as my first film, *Bread and Alley*, the story of a boy who encounters a dog on his way home from the bakery. We took a seven-year-old and a stray dog, neither of whom had any acting experience. The boy is kicking a can while he walks. The can hits the dog, which barks, and the boy runs off. My idea was to have him walk directly in front of the dog, so I bought a bicycle, put it on the opposite side of the street, and told him he could have it if he walked past the animal. It worked perfectly and we both got what we wanted. The trick was to have the child actually experience what his fictional character was going through.

For the scene in *The Traveller* where the boy gets a beating, I asked him what he would take in exchange for actually being caned ten times. He said he wanted a gym suit and a football. Once we started shooting, the truthfulness of the scene startled even me. The woman in the frame really was that boy's mother. She spontaneously turned her head so she couldn't see her son being beaten. It was her honest, human reaction.

There is a scene in *Through the Olive Trees* with Hossein and Mr. Keshavarz sitting in the back of a truck, which stops to pick people up from the side of the road. Mr. Keshavarz asks a young woman if she wants to be in the film. We did three takes. The first one was good because she didn't know what the question was going to be. Her timidity worked wonderfully for the part. By the third take, she knew what the question would be and her shyness had all but vanished. To get the reaction I wanted again, Mr. Keshavarz suddenly asked if she would dance in our film. Watch her eyes when she is asked the question. They go wide and she

hides behind her mother. It was an absolutely genuine reaction. Her spontaneity was sparked. It's a good thing we captured that look when we did because the next question would have been "Will you take your clothes off for the film?"

❀❀❀

A friend of mine was over for dinner and wanted some cigarettes, so my son went out to buy them for her. We waited a long time for him to come back before discovering that he had walked three miles into town to find a pack. That sense of responsibility, the sort of perseverance that should always somehow be rewarded, is what I wanted to convey in *Where is the Friend's House?*

I needed a particular reaction shot from Babak Ahmadpour, the boy in *Where is the Friend's House?*, in the scene near the start of the film, when his mother tells him he is forbidden to go in search of his school friend. He has accidentally placed his friend's notebook in his bag and wants to return it to him. We see the confused look on the boy's face for only a few seconds, but it is something I will never forget. What I did was put him in front of the camera and ask him a maths problem. What looks to us like him wondering why his mother won't let him go is actually him staring into space, doing sums, trying to deal with all those numbers flying through his head.

The boy later finds himself in the dark alleys of an unknown village. He hears a dog barking and is terrified. We don't see the dog, only the look on Babak's face, which I considered a crucially important image that we had to get right because, in a way, the film succeeds or fails because of the expressive eyes of this young boy. Showing that unequivocal look of defiance and perseverance was vital. One of the crew went around the corner and started barking loudly. I turned to my assistant, making sure the boy could hear me, and said, "Are you sure you tied the dog up? Go check to see that it doesn't escape. It's wild, after all. Very dangerous. Give it a bone so it doesn't chew through the rope. We don't want it biting anyone." And so on. Babak was convinced the animal was about to escape and attack him. Much later I added a recording of a real dog to the soundtrack.

In both these cases, giving the boy something concrete to focus on, rather than telling him just to pretend, was a much more effective way of getting what I wanted on film. I even orchestrated certain things a couple of weeks before filming started, including carefully creating a fake classroom situation into which we placed Babak. It meant that from the start he thought he really had taken the notebook of his friend and that we – the film crew – had come from Tehran to help him return it. The crucial thing for Babak was to ensure that the notebook was handed back as soon as possible. Meanwhile, we made a film around him. "Please hurry and find your friend," I told him. "We all have to get home as soon as possible."

❁❁❁

I found the boy who plays the lead in *The Traveller* playing football in a dirt field. In one sequence, I wanted him to stand in front of the goal, play poorly, let the other team score, then have his friend come over and berate him. The moment we started shooting, it became clear that the boy was intent on ignoring me. Whatever I said, he kept on trying his best to catch the ball and prevent the other team from scoring. I took him aside again and again, reminding him that his part required that he let the other team win. Later in the film, the boy and his friend are shown sitting on the front steps of a house. The friend criticises his playing. The boy wouldn't stop arguing, insisting it was his friend who had played badly.

The woman playing the boy's mother in *Where is the Friend's House?* refused to do another take of hand-washing a shirt and hanging it out to dry. She insisted the shirt was clean and that if we needed her to do it again, she was going to get some real dirty laundry. The idea of washing the same clean shirt a second time was inconceivable to her. Eventually my assistant threw the shirt on the ground, saying, "Now it's dirty again!" I wanted to cast one particular boy in the film, but his mother wasn't happy about it. She told us she had once seen a film about a child getting lost and being found only twenty years later. Nothing we could say would convince her that if her son appeared in a film, he would not automatically disappear.

I wanted one of the children in *Where is the Friend's House?* to lie under a desk in the classroom, so I chose a boy who worked delivering heavy crates of milk after school, and who really did have back pain. "When I ask why you are underneath the table," I said to him, "explain that it's because of your back." We set up the camera and the boy got under the table. We rolled the camera and I asked him why he was under there. He poked his head out and said, "You told me to get under here." I asked my assistant to talk with the boy, and even get under the table with him. We went for another take and I asked the same question. The boy pointed to my assistant and said, "He told me to do it!"

The inhabitants of the village where we made *The Wind Will Carry Us* had absolutely no notion of cinema and were wholly preoccupied with their own work. It took much persuading for the father to allow his young son to be in the film. The idea of leaving sheep on their own in the fields was incomprehensible to him. This all worked to our advantage because nobody really understood what we were doing or was bothered by the camera. Many locals turned out to be magnificent actors. In fact, they didn't act at all. They were naturally perfect. After two days of filming with the woman in the coffee shop sequence in *The Wind Will Carry Us*, she told us she wouldn't be able to come back the next day so would send her daughter instead. There was no way to make her understand that it was her we needed. Perhaps if she had understood, she wouldn't have given such a magnificent performance.

❀ ❀ ❀

Art sees things in close-up, focusing our attention, teaching us to not cast blame so freely. Art doesn't make judgements, it informs and teaches. The camera allows truth to circulate in places it might not otherwise go.

❀ ❀ ❀

Emotions should guide the actor's gestures, not the other way around. If you want a performer to be sad, stir up that emotion in him. If a character is fearful, I might try to genuinely frighten the actor playing the part. Everything has to be as real and truthful as possible. Ask a non-professional actor to be happy, and most just smile. Ask him to be sad, and all you get is a scowl. It's all too theatrical and unconvincing. When I work with non-professional actors, I don't want them acting. I need them to be themselves. Discover what pushes someone to behave in a certain way, then take advantage by devising strategies to make it happen.

Kiarostami screens the opening sequence of Ten, *filmed with two cameras attached to the dashboard of a car, with Mania Akbari and her real-life son, playing mother and child, driving through the streets of Tehran. The boy is upset because he doesn't want to miss his swimming race. Later sequences involve Mania giving lifts to a handful of women.*

I spent time with the boy and his mother, getting to know his likes and dislikes. For the sequence where she drives him to the swimming pool, it was important she take the route that really does lead to the pool, otherwise he wouldn't have believed in what was happening. Reality and fiction had to merge, and provide a credible environment for the actors. Every time she deviated, he immediately asked, "Aren't we going to the swimming pool?" and lost his concentration. We filmed the sequence three times, always on a Tuesday, when the boy was scheduled to swim. Mania was sneaky, making sure they left the house late, which upset him,

83

and as soon as they were sitting in the car, she pretended to forget her glasses and wallet, so he was even more agitated. It was risky to work this way because he could have decided he didn't want to be in the film at all.

Shooting lasted three months because we worked only when the atmosphere felt right for the performers, which couldn't be planned in advance, so the car and cameras were always at their disposal. Depending on their availability and, more importantly, how they were feeling, the actors let me know when we should film. Sometimes we worked only one or two days a week. The filmmaker can deliver the script whenever he wants but has to wait for the non-professional performer to tap into emotions in tune with that script. Without this alignment, the performances might not be so believable. There is a real story behind every sad face in my films.

Even if I were somehow guiding the conversations in *Ten*, the actors' words and expressions were their own. Reality was always the starting point. I knew that the woman who played the prostitute had been arguing with her boyfriend in the run-up to filming. I felt this could be useful, as her character in *Ten* isn't a very happy person, and told her to call me whenever she felt like filming. Just before we started shooting, this young woman's relationship with her boyfriend improved, so I asked him to start an argument with her. I knew she would call me and say, "Today's the day. We should film now." This modest and upstanding woman is in reality very different to her onscreen character – I think perhaps she wanted to show her hidden side – thus demonstrating that there are exceptions to the rule that when it comes to hiring actors, you should pick someone as close as possible to the part they are playing. The first take we did of her talking with Mania in the car was out of focus, but it was absolutely the best performance, so we used it anyway.

A woman going out in the evening might put on her makeup a few hours earlier so it blends in with her skin. It's the same with emotions. An actor has to sleep with them so that by morning they truly belong. When the sentiment is right and the dialogue is compelling, the acting is believable.

The manager of a football team knows the individual talents of his players, and long before kick-off draws up a game plan that enables him to use them to his best advantage. But once the whistle blows, he sits on the sidelines and watches. He can light up a cigarette and either take pleasure in the game or get all bent out of shape. During halftime he might offer suggestions, keeping things in check and making adjustments, but his real work – selecting the players, ensuring the right mix of characters, devising tactics – has already been done. The players out on the pitch need that freedom.

During the filming of *Ten* there was no need for an interfering director. I relinquished almost all power and privilege. When shooting, I was sometimes in the back seat of the car, angled so the cameras couldn't see me, and other times was following in a separate car. I was never a commanding presence bellowing instructions. Instead, I just listened, as someone in the audience watching the finished film might do. The boy was left to his own devices and seemed to completely forget about both camera and me, which is what I hoped would happen. I occasionally fed Mania lines through an earpiece, which is why sometimes you see her adjusting her hijab. This gave me a small degree of control, but that was the only directing I did during shooting.

❖ ❖ ❖

We auditioned more than one hundred men for the role of the professor in *Like Someone in Love*, some of whom had made films with Kurosawa and other famous directors. In the end I chose Tadashi Okuno. Working with him was an unmatched experience. For fifty years he earned a living as a film extra and had never once spoken a line of dialogue. I didn't want him to feel intimidated, and told him he had only a small part in the film, perhaps at most a page-and-a-half of dialogue. Every night I would give him scenes for the following day. Towards the middle of the shoot, he mentioned to my interpreter that his role seemed much bigger than I had originally suggested, that I had perhaps stretched the truth. He knew he had been tricked, but was gracious about it nonetheless.

Mr. Okuno possessed certain characteristics similar to the character I had in mind, and the way he played the part is a mixture of my vision and the reality of who he actually is. When he put his slippers on, he glided along in that apartment – which we constructed in the shell of an unfinished building – as if he had been doing it every day for decades. He told me he felt at home whenever he sat at the desk. I complimented the set decorator on a job well done, and he thanked me for finding an actor who fit so well with his design. When we finished filming, I told Mr. Okuno it had been a wonderful experience working with him and that there was another film I wanted to shoot in Japan. He thanked me politely and explained that though touched by my proposal, he didn't want to play a lead role again and would rather go back to his life as an extra. It was Buddha who said, "The wise man never shines." If someone puts himself on display, nobody notices. Remain in the shadows and the whole world opens their eyes. Mr. Okuno is the last samurai.

❀ ❀ ❀

The artist reflects on harrowing experiences without cynicism, thus making it possible for us to draw pleasure from pain, to be enlightened by adversities and calamities. Rumi tells us that if we choose to gaze with grace at something gruesome, we can perceive its glory. Everything depends on how we behold.

❋ ❋ ❋

Clarity is vital. You don't want the audience to feel stupid. Make sure everything can be understood. Intrigue your audience. Inject ambiguities. Create multi-dimensional characters and complex situations. But never leave anyone confused.

❋ ❋ ❋

An experiment is always worth attempting.

❋ ❋ ❋

People say I make films for children. I have actually made only one film for children, a short entitled *Colours*. Many of the rest are about children. The fact that so many of my films feature children doesn't mean they are directed towards them as an audience.

An Arab proverb tells us there are four elements that differentiate a child from an adult. The child has no instinct for possession or preservation, has no notion of hatred when arguing, accords no importance to external appearances, and is prone to being relatively unrestrained when it comes to revealing his emotions. Children, in general, have a freer outlook on life. They don't complicate things. They have no ulterior motives and are rarely conscious of how they look and sound to the world. They don't play games in front of the camera. They don't need a cup of coffee every morning and don't think about money or celebrity. They take no notice of conventions and traditions. Children remind adults that we should be continually astonished at the world around us, that we shouldn't look at life with such indifference, that we should open our eyes and revel in the moment. Children are so receptive, so mischievous, always articulating themselves with stunning clarity. Ask a question and listen to their extraordinary responses. They remind me of the Sufi mystics who live constantly in the here and now. I have learned so much from children. They teach adults indirectly about how to communicate with people as transparently as possible and how to curb pessimism. Being able to keep your mouth shut can be useful. If I hadn't worked with children early in my career, I would probably have developed into a very different sort of filmmaker.

As for working with children as actors, they bring a simplicity and libertine sense of playfulness to the screen if you let them be themselves. To draw out the best performance from a child, act alongside them. Become a child yourself and re-discover yourself – your infant state, that unselfconsciousness, those childlike sensibilities – through them. The children in my films have all been headstrong and independent, always coming up with ideas more interesting than Marlon Brando ever could. But sometimes they haven't even known I was directing them. That's how I was able to get those performances. *First Graders* is full of interviews with children going to school for the first time, suddenly thrown into a world where they are bound by rigid rules. When the children arrived in class on the first day of school, a week before we started filming, they saw the blackboard, desks, benches and – in clear view – a camera on a tripod. We never told them not to look at it because that would have been the best way to ensure that they did just that. As it was a new environment for the children, the camera was just another object, the cameraman just another person – a figure of authority – in the room. We filmed without a clapperboard, which helped to maintain concentration. This meant issues with synchronisation during editing, but it was worth it. When the children spoke, it really was them talking, in their own voices, without my intervention.

The most important thing is that children don't feel that you, the filmmaker, are judging them, that you feel more important than them. They can immediately sense if you are doing this, and will resist your presence. Akira Kurosawa once asked me how I got the performances I did from children. "They seem so at ease in front of your camera," he said. I explained that I never talk down to them, that I don't appear to be in charge, that the children don't even know I'm the director. To communicate effectively with a child, you have to adjust yourself to their level and speak in their language. Once contact has been made, there is no need to order them to do anything. By letting them express whatever they want at that moment, I get what I am looking for. The same rapport is usefully adopted for older lay performers, and even some professional actors.

❁ ❁ ❁

To enjoy something I have to be intrigued. And only novelty intrigues me. Experience and continual learning draw my attention. I'm still learning. Of course I am. It's a lifelong quest. Beware of definitive judgements.

❀ ❀ ❀

Artists yearn to communicate. That's what makes them artists. They become sick if they are unable to share their dreams.

❀ ❀ ❀

Sit on a bench in a public park and start selling real paintings by Picasso for a few pennies each. See if you manage to get rid of a single one. Most people want simplicity when watching a film. They want something immediately comprehensible. They resent paying for something they don't understand.

❀ ❀ ❀

The indirect aim of creating art is to retreat deep into childhood games. That's where real joy lies. As soon as a child discovers something he wants to achieve beyond the sheer pleasure of the game itself, the moment he becomes competitive, the game is over. At its best, artistic work is a childlike process where elements of the unconscious grow in strength, eventually overwhelming the conscious. Re-connecting with youthful impulses isn't a choice for an artist. It's a necessity.

I'm glad there are no grown-ups in my life telling me what to do. These days, when I spend time with my family and they start talking about one thing or another, often I take my leave and join the children in the other room. I find most adult conversations uninteresting. The most wondrous period in the life of a human being is childhood, when encountering even the most minuscule things becomes a process of radical exploration. It's a pity we leave those times behind so quickly. For most people, unfortunately, removing ourselves – even hastening our departure – from that state of awareness, is the most natural thing. As the years and decades move on, stages of life reveal themselves. Early on, we think we know everything. Then comes a period of worry and doubt, after which is a phase when we actively seek to rekindle the experiences of childhood. This third and final stage is where I have been for some time now.

❀ ❀ ❀

During auditions, I tell the prospective actor a joke and ask him to tell it to someone else. Can he play the game?

❀ ❀ ❀

When it comes to selecting actors, instinct and gut response are usually reliable. Once filming starts, the first take is usually the best. If you have to discuss specific lines and how they should be played, or find yourself having to carefully block the actors in front of the camera, the spontaneity that might otherwise have been there drops away. If we have to do more than three takes, if an actor is struggling with the dialogue, if he is being pulled too far from his true character, I begin to question my approach. By the time I stand next to the camera, looking out on the actors, it should be clear how to get what I need. If it doesn't happen almost immediately and spontaneously, it's a case of going back to the drawing board. Filming is halted and I re-think things.

Anyone can be an actor, provided the character he plays corresponds sufficiently to his innermost being. You can't fundamentally change the way a non-professional approaches a role, so make sure you choose the right person for the job. If who you are working with isn't sufficiently similar to the character you have in mind, quickly adapt and change. Set the camera and lights around the actors, not the other way round, then marvel at how much information lay performers can convey with such little effort.

Working with non-professionals can be arduous. Most need to be handled delicately. It's like a chemical formula. Too much of one element and not enough of another, and the whole thing blows up in your face. Some want to know if the character they are playing is sympathetic or not, whether they will be looked upon as being either a positive or negative figure. To answer that question definitively will almost certainly affect the way someone approaches a role, so I try not to discuss specifics. There are no explanations from me, no unnecessary information. On the other

90

hand, you won't believe how easy it can be if you get the casting right. Non-professional actors might be able to play only one role: themselves. But some play it stunningly well.

⚙ ⚙ ⚙

Every character in a film is important. Don't think just anyone can play a role because it's a small one. A bad performance, of whatever length, can affect every frame in the audience's mind and leave a hole at the centre of a film. Don't permit a single false note to develop.

⚙ ⚙ ⚙

Something almost unnoticeable – like the sudden imperceptible blink of an eye – can make the difference between a good take and a bad one, animating me as a filmmaker and providing the necessary energy to continue. The fisherman makes plans but never knows exactly what he will uncover in his catch. The net is full of surprises. I delight when the unexpected supersedes planning. Curiosity, improvisation, randomness. We search for happy accidents.

Many ideas appear on my doorstep, some more forcefully than others, but most disappear just as quickly. Only the strongest remain. My initial story ideas are sometimes no more than half a page. If I can develop those paragraphs into three pages, I suspect the idea is robust enough for a full-length film. But when a script becomes too detailed – if I can fully visualise the images and hear the dialogue to the point where it feels limiting – then I don't have much inclination to turn it into a film, so might hand it over to a colleague.

"I can't do this," the cameraman of one of my early films told me on the third day of working together. "When I arrive on set I need to know where to put the lights. I need a shooting script." I didn't have one, so that evening spent several hours writing out the following day's shots. My plan for the first sequence involved a close-up on the main character, but when I arrived on set the next day it was clear the actor wasn't in the right mood, so there and then I decided to change things. The cameraman was grateful when I handed him the shooting script, but by skipping that first shot we were back to square one. It was clear I would never be able to make a film based on a document like that. The emotions and feelings an actor has in the moment, while on set, interacting with others, are of more concern to me than a detailed breakdown of shots prepared the night before. The screenplay provides no more than a foundation on which we build. Beware of commitment to anything written.

Sit quietly. Just sit quietly. And an idea will come to you.

I expect little return on my work, either financial or critical. There have been several books written about my films, but I have read none of them, and I don't read reviews. I would never say that I don't care whether people like my films or not, but I can tell you that their liking what I do doesn't affect my own feelings about it. I'm not troubled when someone tells me they don't understand something I have created. There seems to be enough appreciation of my films for me to know that they aren't entirely incomprehensible.

When people hear I won the Palme d'Or at Cannes and see that my films aren't playing in the local multiplex, and that certain critics like my work, their first thought is that my cinema must be overwhelmingly convoluted. But their expectations are often overturned and they are genuinely surprised when they come to see that my work is actually quite simple. The scene in all my films that provokes the most queries is the shot near the start of *Close-Up* of a can rolling down a street. The number of theories I have heard about that single moment! People don't believe me when I explain where this image came from. They expect something terribly profound, but the truth is there was a slope in front of the house where we were filming. The important events of the story were taking place inside and I wanted to represent the inactivity of the man standing outside. I created a scene where he would cause an empty spray can to roll gently down the hill. I just liked the image and figured I wouldn't have many other opportunities to capture a shot like that, one I knew would somehow get audiences involved. We also had time to kill and a few feet of film in the camera. A deadly combination.

❧ ❧ ❧

I have long since known that I am not suited to the world of film festivals, to that sort of life. Being on display, having to proclaim on things – including my own work – is disquieting for me. The idea of doing the work, then putting it on a shelf, without showing it to anyone, of expending no energy on placing it before the gaze of an audience, is quietly appealing. At the same time, the best thing, when I do go to festivals, isn't the films I might see but the possibility of meeting someone new. The right human encounter has always reaffirmed my faith.

❧ ❧ ❧

I can understand if someone walks out twenty minutes into one of my films. I can also understand if someone stays twenty minutes after the end.

It has been said that a director should have a basic understanding – even some experience – of acting. I agree, though I am certainly no great actor and have never felt comfortable in front of the camera. I once filmed myself when I made a film about schoolchildren. It wasn't easy for me, and I decided I would never do it again. Because of the dark glasses I always wear people said I looked like a thug or a police inspector interrogating children, even a mafioso. I have been interviewed on film more times than I can remember and appear as myself in *10 on Ten*, but more interesting to me are the occasions when I have acted alongside the characters in my films. For *Taste of Cherry* I sat inside the car talking to the person next to me while filming him, which was acting of a sort. I pretended to be someone other than I am because, for those moments, my job was to draw genuine responses from the actors that could be recorded and used in an entirely different context.

Kiarostami screens several scenes of the film, the central character of which is a middle-aged man named Badii, played by Homayoun Ershadi. By the end of Badii's search for someone to assist him in his suicide, as he drives around Tehran and the hills outside the city, he has spoken to three men of different ages and social standing: a young soldier, a seminarian and an elderly taxidermist.

The film was made in such a way that Ershadi never actually met any of the people he has in his car. Look again and you'll see that Badii never appears in the same shot as those three characters. Whenever one of them is on screen, I was on the other side of the camera, responding, eliciting specific reactions and lines of dialogue from him. When you see Ershadi, I was sitting in the passenger seat, operating the camera – which was attached to the door – and talking to him. When you see one of the three men in the passenger seat, I was driving, talking and operating. It was only ever just the actor and me in the car. We weren't being towed and there was no big crew waiting to jump in as soon as the car stopped. Apart from the sound engineer, who was on the roof, everyone was far away, drinking tea. I knew it was risky to shoot the entire film from such a small number of angles, but I didn't want to put the camera on the hood of the car. Almost the entirety of *Taste of Cherry* is a construct, a series of intercut single shots. Even near the end, when Badii steps out of his car and talks to the taxidermist, we never see them together in the same shot.

"How is it you look like that in the film?" the elderly actor asked me after watching the sequence in which he appears. "So different from what I remember." Thanks to the momentum of the editing and emotional force of the storytelling, audiences never consider this a shortcoming, and as far as I can tell, most viewers never even notice they aren't watching an actual conversation between two people.

Ask a non-professional to speak for the camera and he stiffens up. But if what you ask him to do is so pressing and urgent and interesting to him, he forgets we are making a film. The key is to instil confidence so that the actor – professional or amateur – trusts you, no matter what. Part of my job as a director is to trick him into doing what is needed. Some people, if they know exactly what's going on – that I am out to get them to perform – fall apart in front of the camera. Is what I do insensitive and manipulative? Perhaps, but manipulation isn't always a bad thing. It has always been a valid way to capture truth on film.

For a couple of weeks before the shoot I met with Afshin Khorshid Bakhtiari, a labourer who plays the soldier, and had him do various odd jobs, paying a wage he could expect. He would fix the car, clean up the house and water the garden, things like that. I needed to establish a connection with him, some level of trust. I occasionally mentioned the film I was making and that I wanted him involved, that there was a specific job I wanted him for, but maintained a certain distance, so I didn't have to answer too many questions. He was forever asking me precisely what was required of him, but I was especially vague. Eventually we bought a uniform for him, which he wasn't happy about because he thought we were trying to enlist him in the army. He refused to have a haircut but I persuaded him to get a trim, and when he was sitting in the barber's chair I told them to cut it all off. He basically had no comprehension of filmmaking, or even of cinema. When it came to filming in the car, he saw the camera but didn't really understand what it was we were doing.

Nothing was rehearsed. I told him he would get paid if he drove around with me, answering my questions and talking. I spoke spontaneously, with the hope that he would start warming to the conversation. Then, in the middle of a sentence, as we started on the subject I wanted him to talk about, I switched on the camera. He responded with dialogue based on my questions, but at all times with his own feelings and thoughts. His responses were his own, though I gently pushed him towards saying certain things I thought would be useful for the film. Sometimes I asked him the same question more than once, each time saying, "Sorry, I didn't hear you. Could you tell me again?"

I told him about the specific job I wanted him for only when I was certain I had everything else I needed him to say on film, at which point I opened up, explaining that I wanted him to assist with my suicide. You can see how uncomfortable he becomes as the car moves further and further up into the hills, away from the city. At one point, I spoke to him using the few words of Czech I know, which prompted from him a look of utter confusion, then asked him to get my cigarettes from the glove compartment. Inside was a large knife covered with pomegranate juice, the colour of blood. His reaction – that fear on his face – is genuine, as is the shot of him running from the car. I would have liked a few more minutes of him reacting to the situation, but if he had seen me change reels and ask the same questions again, the whole thing would probably have fallen apart. I couldn't have expected that same response a second time.

I encountered Mir-Hossein Noori, who plays the seminarian, in my neighbourhood, where there is a theological seminary. Sometimes, when I walk past the front gate, I stop and play a game with myself: I tell myself I will make a film starring the first person who walks out. I stood there, a couple of weeks before the filming of *Taste of Cherry* began, looking intently through the door frame, when I heard a voice from behind. "Excuse me," said Noori as he walked past carrying a bag of fresh bread. I immediately knew I had found my actor. When it came to filming, he was anxious to talk and let his feelings be known because he thought I really did want to commit suicide. I suggested we discuss certain things, though at all times he used his own words. Although Noori was an earnest student at the time, a few years later he married a Swedish woman, became a filmmaker, and left his religious studies behind.

I found the old man – Abdolrahman Bagheri, a taxi driver – up in the hills where we filmed. "What are you doing here?" he asked. It looked obvious to me because we were carrying so much camera equipment. "You're a bunch of thieves," he insisted, "the usual speculators from the city here to measure and divide up the territory, then sell it to developers. You suck the lifeblood from this land." I liked the tone and expression of the way he spoke to us, and immediately knew I wanted him for the film. I asked if he would work with us for the next three or four days, starting tomorrow. "I can't," he said. "I have to fix my car. The tires are all worn out." I told him we would give him four new tires if he showed up tomorrow, sat in a car with me, and repeated what he just said about the land. When he left, I had my assistant follow, just in case he decided not to show up. Bagheri came back the next day and agreed to be in the film, saying, "I spoke to my daughter, who saw an interview you gave on television and says you are an important man." Bagheri was the only one I gave the script to. He was happy with all but a couple of pages, which were about divorce. I explained that my ideas on the subject were influenced by reality. "That doesn't mean we have to talk about them," he said. I tore up those pages. It's important to know when to heed someone's innermost convictions, when they truly need to be listened to.

Bagheri had some sort of authority over me. He was like a human air conditioner, able to express his philosophy of life – about our right to die as an expression of free will – in a gloriously unintellectual way, bringing freshness and weight to the film. Bagheri and Noori touch on the same ideas in their conversations and both sympathise with Ershadi's character, but while Noori explains that he hasn't actually lived through certain things, that he knows about them only because of his studies and thoughtful contemplation, it's immediately clear that Bagheri has

lived through a great deal and has an instinctive understanding of the world through direct experience. An inanimate book has less impact than someone standing before us, talking and drawing inspiration from his own joys and struggles.

I filmed the young labourer first, then looked carefully at the footage, after which I filmed Ershadi, who filled in the gaps, with me in the passenger seat. I did the same with the other two, then pieced everything together. Filming took about six weeks, longer than normal for me because we shot for only two or three hours a day, always in the late afternoon when sunlight was fading. Listen carefully and you will notice very few moments when there is overlapping dialogue. It's all put together very precisely. Everything you hear is intentional, including street noises and sirens.

I searched for someone to play the part of Badii for nearly a year. Then I saw Homayoun Ershadi – a professional architect – driving through Tehran, and knocked on his car window as he sat at a traffic light. I spent six months with him before we started shooting, during which time we never talked about the film as such, though from time to time discussed his character. I just wanted to get to know him. Instead of asking him to read a script and discuss it with me, I showed him an hour-long videotape my son and I had made of me driving around those same hills above Tehran, talking spontaneously to the camera, footage containing many of the ideas that ended up in the finished film. It meant that when we started filming there was no need to tell Ershadi precisely how he should be feeling or what emotions he should be acting out. All he had to do was bring to mind what he had absorbed from this tape, putting himself in my place. I was able to direct him by conditioning him not through written words but by means of images and spoken dialogue. Showing him the footage helped him preserve a certain naturalness. There was no need for him to adapt himself to a written text that he might have learned by heart but never quite managed to make his own, then struggle to distance himself from.

Ershadi turned out to be a rather unhappy person. When I first asked if he wanted to be in the film, he said he would be delighted, but did so with absolutely no expression on his face. I realised he was already in tune with Badii. During filming, I was careful not to get him too excited because I didn't want to pull him out of that state. His low mood was vital to the success of his performance and the film. I even spread devious rumours that I knew would get back to Ershadi. One time I told the crew I didn't think he was doing a very good job, and asked the sound recordist to play him a tape we had made of me expressing my faked dissatisfaction.

❀ ❀ ❀

I don't know if I have the audacity to make a film like *Taste of Cherry* again. The bravery just isn't in me anymore. I particularly like the series of shots near the end, just before Badii climbs into the grave, of him walking from his car and sitting, overlooking the landscape, smoking a cigarette. It lasts two and half minutes. Who knows if I have the nerve to do that sort of thing again? Audiences these days seem so impatient.

❀ ❀ ❀

Reaction is as important as action. The image of someone responding – even silently – to what is being said can be more significant than what is said. For this reason, the recitation of dialogue I have written is less exciting to me than watching creative actors react to those words. The only part of the process I have limited prior knowledge of, that I am unable to foresee, that I cannot predict, happens at the moment of performance. Watching the intuitive reactions of one actor to words spoken by another is what thrills me, even more so than the articulation of well-rehearsed lines.

The process of turning an idea into a film can be a long and arduous one. The heaviest burden rests not on the cameraman or soundman or set designer, not even on the director, but on the actor. No one else can transform a script into a film the way an actor does. There are many important decisions that can't be made without the actor's input. If you allow yourself to be directed by actors, rather than the other way round, the end result will be more interesting. This all became clear to me when I started working with children. By all means guide them, but also let them direct themselves. As a filmmaker, one of the important things I learned from time spent with children is adjusting myself to working within a set of circumstances that offers few clues about what might happen next. Rigidity is the enemy of spontaneity and the imagination.

✿✿✿

In auditions I measure the confidence of non-professionals. It's important to know if someone will be able to deliver what I need, whether he can perform on screen. We sit and talk, then I turn on the camera without him knowing. After a few minutes, once he and I are absorbed in conversation, I pretend to switch on the camera. Later, when I watch the tape, if there is no difference between the moments before and after the pretend switch is flicked, there is a chance this person will be able to ignore the machinery of film production and be himself on screen. As in real life, when it comes to selecting actors you can quickly tell who is a time-waster.

✿✿✿

Can a character appear more interesting if we only ever see him in the dark?

✿✿✿

I enjoy looking at someone and trying to guess what is going on in his mind.

✿✿✿

With filmmaking comes the challenges of production, of finding locations, of investing time in casting, of bringing together a crew. An ambush lies around every corner. All said and done, it's a miracle that anything other than the prosaic ends up in a finished film. If you can achieve even a single poetic image, consider yourself fortunate.

✿✿✿

If you want to draw a believable performance from an actor, put something into his hands. Distract him from his dialogue. With something else to focus on, something physical, the lines come out more naturally.

That's a real teacher talking to a class of real students in the opening sequence of *Where is the Friend's House?* I spent a few days with him before we shot the scene. Although he was a rather stiff character when walking through the school corridors, he

101

came alive the moment he began interacting with children in the classroom. It was fascinating to watch, as if he were an actor who had mastered one role in his life: that of a teacher. Unfortunately he reverted to his usual stiff self in front of the camera. He was in his element in the classroom, but having me in the room was a problem for him, and also for me, because I wasn't able to direct him in any substantive way in front of the children. I had to respect his position of authority and take him outside to tell him certain things, which broke the momentum of filming. To loosen him up I gave him as many physical things to do as I could think of, like fiddling with the door so it wouldn't stay shut, which meant he had to keep walking over to close it. In the film, as soon as he enters the room, he throws down the piece of paper he has in his hand, goes over to close the window, then takes off his jacket.

Occasionally, you have to be more mischievous. The children's faces make it clear they aren't acting in that scene. Something more serious was going on. I needed Ahmad Ahmadpour, who plays Mohamed, to deliver specific lines while crying, so a week before we shot the scene I asked one of my assistants to take a photo of Ahmad and give it to him. He was excited and loved having this Polaroid. Everyone complimented him on it, telling him how good he looked and how proud he should be of it. I told him to keep hold of it and not let anyone take another photo of him. "Don't show it to anyone," I said. "Everyone else will want one too." Behind the boy's back I asked the photographer to take a second photo of Ahmad and at the same time reassure him, saying that Mr. Kiarostami would never know about it.

A couple of days later, I went to Ahmad and told him I knew he had allowed himself to be photographed. "Don't let it happen again," I said. We did this a second time, which meant there was now a third photograph, which the photographer told Ahmad to hide between the pages of his exercise book. When I confronted the boy and found the third photo, I tore it up in front of him. He began to cry, and with the camera rolling I said, "How many times have I told you not to let anyone else take a photo of you?" Ahmad tearfully responded with "Three times." I replaced my voice on the soundtrack with the teacher asking, "How many times have I told you to write your homework in your notebook?" The hand you see in the shot is mine, not the teacher's. He wasn't even in the room at the time.

This is the sort of devious behaviour I spend time convincing myself is all for a good cause. So long as the film is worthy, the ends apparently justify the means. A few days later, we took plenty of photos of Ahmad and gave them to him, which made him very happy. Children are so resilient.

❖ ❖ ❖

We filmed *Where is the Friend's House?* in a remote area, working with children who had never seen a single film, which made the job relatively easy. Today, there are television screens and cameras everywhere. You have only to think about the children in *ABC Africa* who stare into the lens and leap up and down with excitement, ecstatic in the knowledge that they are being filmed, to understand the all-pervasive influence of the moving image. Someone with no knowledge of the camera isn't afraid because he attaches no importance to it. Making *Where is the Friend's House?* and *ABC Africa* would be more difficult today.

❖ ❖ ❖

If there is anything enigmatic and challenging about my films, it is enigmatic and challenging for everyone, not just non-Iranians.

❖ ❖ ❖

I don't write much down before visiting the places where I plan to film. If a scene I am thinking about requires there be a door that someone walks through, I first find a location that contains a real door, then proceed accordingly. Casting that door is just as important as finding the right actors. The filming location, the spaces through which the actors move, are as important as anything else.

❖ ❖ ❖

In the last shot of *Where is the Friend's House?*, Ahmad's teacher finds a flower pressed into the notebook, the flower given to Ahmad by the old man the night before. That moment always has a strong impact on audiences, as well as on me when I first thought of it. I wasn't able to write down anything myself when

I first started thinking about the film because I had injured my hand, so I dictated my ideas to a friend, who could never keep up and was always begging me to go slower. I suddenly thought of that last shot of the flower. The image just appeared in my mind. "Quick," I told my friend, "write this down! Quickly! This is important!" Whenever I see that image, I can't stop smiling.

❀ ❀ ❀

Boris puts Kiarostami's ideas into practice. With his seven-year-old nephew, Erik, as lead actor, he devises a light-hearted story about a boy demanding payment from those wanting entry to a public lift, to be shot in the block where he lives. Boris casts Presley, another workshop participant, as the person who eventually throws Erik out of the building. For the climax, when Presley insists that the boy leave, Boris shoots only Presley's lines. He doesn't turn the camera around to film Erik's reactions and dialogue because he has already spent the morning getting the required close-ups from the boy. By asking Erik questions totally unrelated to the script, a sincere emotional response to Presley's lines was printed to videotape two hours ago, to be intercut later with his questions.

❀ ❀ ❀

I should thank so many of you for not shooting hand-held. God blesses those filmmakers who use tripods.

❀ ❀ ❀

I have bad hearing in my right ear. This minor malady can be useful because I am able to turn my bad ear in the direction of my mother whenever she nags me. It's good to be able to block certain things from my consciousness, to have as much control over what I hear as over what I see.

❀ ❀ ❀

The iris in my left eye never closes and lets in too much light. I can't stop seeing. I don't take my dark glasses off for anyone. By now no one would know me without them.

Those who love life dwell on what comes after. Death enables us to take hold of life, to accept responsibility for our existence. The desire to do away with oneself has crossed many minds, including my own. Every morning we ask ourselves one question: why should I live? We don't choose our race, nationality, religion, father, mother or the colour of our skin. The only thing we are able to choose freely is whether or not we want to live. The possibility of suicide is our only real freedom, an exit from this world. If we don't exercise this freedom it is because – in spite of all difficulties – we have decided to stay alive. When we accept the fact that we have chosen to live and when we come to terms with this freedom, we live more joyously. Philosophy and art teach us that life is not imposed upon us, it is being offered. We have been handed an entrance ticket, but also an exit ticket, which sits folded in our pocket. If you don't like one of my films, you are free to take the door marked "EXIT." Apparently Nietzsche wrote that if someone is standing next to a pit preparing himself to jump in, we should give them a helpful push.

◈ ◈ ◈

The shape of *Taste of Cherry* is drawn from a Persian poem about a butterfly that flies around a candle, moving closer and closer to the flame until it burns. In the film, Badii drives around in his car until he falls into the grave he has dug for himself. The story was also inspired by the tale of a man being chased by a lion. To save himself, he is forced to jump off a cliff, but gets caught on the root of a plant growing out of the side of the mountain. He finds himself between the enormous chasm below and the ferocious beast stalking him above. Just then he notices two mice – one white, one black – gnawing at the root he is hanging from. In the midst of this alarming situation, he sees a strawberry growing on the mountainside, and in that precarious situation, fraught with danger and uncertainty, he reaches out, picks the strawberry, and eats it. When we awoke this morning our deaths were further away than they are now. Do all you can to enjoy life.

The world will outlast any individual destiny. That leaf sitting on the tree branch will one day be carried away by the wind. A writer recently committed suicide in Iran. She was found in a forest, her body at the end of a rope. There was a photo. If you looked to one side you could see the world – birds, nature, beauty – going on as usual. The eternal endures. We are transitory. Anything else is vanity.

❀ ❀ ❀

I don't want to hear this "if a camera is available" from anyone. Make sure a camera is available. Get outside and use it. Each of you should bring into this room, every single day of this workshop, a five-minute scene created with two or three actors, either improvising or using a script, or both, filmed with a single camera, shot in three hours and edited in four. Or just bring in the unedited material to show us. No more excuses.

❀ ❀ ❀

Some of you probably have ideas in mind but don't consider them sufficiently robust. In two days time, without a better idea to work with, you might fall back on your first idea, the one rattling around your head today. I say to you now: get on with exploring this idea today. Don't let your thoughts – your endless processing of the world around you, your worries about how good the result will be – inhibit you. This small film, this experiment, will pave the way for more expansive and expressive ideas. Go outside and get a shot you like – a single image – and build a film around it. Film anything at all. You can decide what it means afterwards. Just get to work. Subject what you create to understanding and consciousness only afterwards. An illegible scribble is still something. Use this time to discover whether you are a filmmaker or not, whether you should consecrate yourself to this profession. Are you the person standing safe on the shore who stares out into dark night, or is that you at sea, amid whirling water? If you discover nothing this week other than the answer to that question, it will have been worthwhile.

In Iran, when I run these workshops, we often travel outside Tehran as a group. The one condition imposed upon everyone is that we talk only about our work, our film projects. Nothing else is discussed. If you do that yourself, today and tomorrow, you will find ideas hiding behind every door. You – not me – are the fuel that will power the next few days. There isn't much I can do if you don't push our time together in specific directions. If you produce no work, I have nothing to respond to. The fact is, I am also here to make films. I always end up with at least one film of my own during these workshops, but because you are all still here instead of outside working, I can't go and work on my project, which I have been mulling over in my mind for a couple of days now. Do anything, even something you feel is useless. It's better than nothing. If you aren't going to make a film for yourself, make one for me. I want out of this room. I refuse to leave here empty-handed.

❀❀❀

In Persian, the words for "slogan" and "poem" are similar. But, of course, they have very different meanings. Some people find political sloganeering more useful than poetry. Not me. There is honesty and sensitivity in a good poem. We can each of us discover ourselves in it. Slogans and political rallying cries – every one of them – are empty. As an artist, don't invest yourself in politics. Those who do are stricken with falsity and impurity. They moan and complain. The futility of it all quickly overwhelms. It's the political crises of our world that help me appreciate the beauties of nature, which is a wholly different and far healthier realm.

❀❀❀

Don't shy away from what you fear is a cliché. A familiar idea can always be re-framed in a novel way.

❀❀❀

These days I require very little. For some years now, I have been ridding myself of almost everything I own. All the awards, trophies, certificates and trinkets I have ever been given were gathering dust in a box in my home, so I handed it over to the film museum in Tehran. All meaningless, as far as I can see, though it's best not to be completely dismissive of such things. After all, some of these pieces of metal and hunks of glass come with cash prizes attached. Money can sometimes be useful in my business. Apply graciousness when necessary.

Every time I serve on a film festival jury, I promise myself I will never do it again. You won't believe this, but from here I go to a festival where I will be on the jury. Who knows why I agreed to go? Perhaps because I enjoy travelling. I find myself abandoning routines and habits when I leave home, which is important to me.

Judging a work of art is a meaningless exercise. What criteria and standards could possibly be brought to bear? For a weightlifter it's the heaviness of the weights and for a runner it's timing. I judge a piece of work based on nothing other than my own tastes. One memory I have is of a festival where I felt that a film was particularly worthy. I wanted it to win something, and it did pick up an award, but the moment the prize was announced I thought to myself, "What have I done? What about the other films? How ridiculous of me to compare one film to another."

Winning an award can be deadly. You hold your head high, but all the while know it's really for naught. The awards I have been handed are a big haze in my mind. When I received them I was flattered, but wondered if I really was worthy. With adulation comes a form of emptiness, even a curious form of dejection. There is little reason to feel pride if your film is selected to be screened at a festival and no reason to feel shame if it isn't. Can anyone other than you determine the true value of your work? The great god of cinema could descend and designate a film a certified masterpiece, but that still wouldn't make it any good. What troubles me is that the demands of festival juries require us to make up our minds there and then. Having to rely on an immediate response is a deceptive way of judging something. It takes time to develop an honest and meaningful relationship with a piece of art. Whether a film stays with you over time is a much more useful determination of its quality, which is why we should be forced to wait ten years before making an assessment.

Rumi writes of two kinds of scholars: those who seek the favour of princes and will do anything to please, and those who follow their instincts, seek the truth for its own sake, and by doing so inspire the people they come into contact with. Do nothing on anyone else's terms.

It requires more precision to tell a story in five shots than in twenty.

Bewilderment can be more exciting than understanding.

It hadn't rained for a few days before I left Tehran to fly here. Water was scarce. I was unable to take a shower, and ended up spending an hour to clean myself using water I had stored up. Later, when I was eventually able to take a shower, it was so pleasurable I felt as if this were the first shower I had ever had. Not being able to take a shower for such a long time meant I was able to fully appreciate the hot water, which I had taken for granted.

110

When something is removed, its reappearance is welcomed more fervently. Rumi tells us that hunger isn't such a bad thing because it makes everything that comes after taste as sweet as can be. In a film, the omission of something – its absence and then reappearance – can make a stronger impact than if it stays in the frame the whole time. What is light without darkness? There is a sequence in *ABC Africa* inspired by my captivating drives through the absolute darkness of the continent. A black screen remains for a full minute before we see the striking of a match, then black again, which is broken only by lightning in the sky. Finally, we see trees blowing in the wind. When there is nothing to look at, nothing to see, what does finally appear has profound power. Punctuate a prolonged silence with sound and the audience pays attention. When we look at nothingness, we sense that something is about to bloom before our eyes. A plant might not have fully emerged from the ground, but we know there are roots growing ever deeper. Something down there is ready to erupt.

A story full of calm allows us to appreciate those moments when something frantic happens, which is why American films have so little impact on me. Everything is in a constant state of flux, with things revealed before anyone has a genuine desire to see them. In *The Wind Will Carry Us* very little occurs while the film crew is in the village, which means some sort of expectation is created in the mind of the audience. "Something has to happen," we tell ourselves. A man trapped in a well – a man we never see – becomes a major event. Establish a sense of emptiness, and a single moment of action can have tremendous significance. Some months ago, I was in a building in northern Iran, where every hallway was narrow and windowless. Then, after three floors of this uniformity, I stepped in front of a vast window that looked out over the sea and a wide, brilliant blue sky. It was a view that moved me tremendously. The impact of this window was even more acute because of the three floors of enclosed spaces.

"I do not complain about your absence," writes Hafez. "There would be no pleasure in your presence were it not for your absence." When we don't see someone for a while, her return feels truly special. We look at nature and say it feels wild and cruel because of the dark and cold, but the mix of hot summer days and bitter winter nights is what makes nature beautiful. The things we dislike don't mean much when uncoupled from the things we love. If we take pleasure in studying daybreak, we also have to find beauty in sunsets. Moments of serenity are strongly felt, but sometimes even more so when that tranquillity is ended. The intensity of such things lies in the power of contrast. Show an empty space to someone and they are immediately receptive. They want to know who or what is about to fill it.

❁ ❁ ❁

I like winter. I find the bracing cold comforting and enlivening. Other seasons arrive at a much slower pace, but in a single sweep, a snowstorm – a coup d'état of whiteness – changes a landscape entirely. The world loses its detail when covered with snow. A new, minimalist beauty is revealed.

❁ ❁ ❁

Truth is ever-changing and can't be fully materialised on film. It remains hidden in the nature of things. What the filmmaker does is expose the concealed in his own particular way.

❁ ❁ ❁

I was born in a country that is perpetually flooded with light. Sometimes the light is "right," sometimes "wrong." Perhaps "adequate" and "inadequate" are the words I should use. I might walk ninety-nine times through a landscape and see nothing special. But then, as I cross a plain for the hundredth time, the light might render something new and special to my eye, if only for a moment. Sometimes I think about how it might be if I could somehow attenuate sunlight, if I could turn it down or adjust it, if I could choose how intense I want the sunshine to be.

❁ ❁ ❁

If you see a film and dislike a specific image it contains, cut it from your mind. Focus only on what you like. Halfway through a film I once watched, there was a shot in which a great deal was happening. I focused on one particular thing and framed it as a close-up in my mind, which made the whole experience more interesting. Create the film you want to see based on what the filmmaker is offering.

A filmmaker sometimes destroys his ideas rather than letting them guide him.

Would I make films even if no one watched them? Would you get up in the morning if you were only person on the planet?

We adjust our public persona depending on whom we speak to. The laundryman in my neighbourhood knows me as Ali Mouri. Even before I give him my clothes to be washed, he rolls his eyes and says, "I know, I know. This all has to be ready today. You're in a hurry." He knows me as a disorganised man about to leave town that very day, so needs his clean clothes immediately.

Consider a character suffering from anxiety. What image can you create to represent that emotion? No dialogue.

I like to include in my films those things that usually end up on the cutting room floor.

Each of us sees God differently. Some prophets evoke a vengeful and pitiless God, others a merciful one. It was the latter that was revealed to us at school, as we learned to write our first words: water, bread, father. The God I have held within since I was five years old is compassionate and kindly.

Day four.
A group walks with Abbas to the museum across the road where two glass elevators stand side by side.

It's a good place to shoot. Come tomorrow with a camera. The mechanism of these lifts, as they move up and down, makes for an interesting image.

"Now all we need is an idea."

Yes. Let's take a look at the elevator in my hotel.

En route, someone asks: "Is the starting point for you the word or the image?"

The image is at the heart of everything I do. A film rooted in images is of more interest to me than one told through narration. A good film is one where, if a viewer were to blink for even a split second, he would miss something important. When we recall our dreams, we think of images not words. Our conception of Heaven or Hell is first and foremost a visual, not verbal, one. We picture angels and devils before we understand their function or meaning. When you smell something, it is immediately transformed into an image, one pulled from the collection in your mind, like the smell of fish conjuring up an image of the sea. When I think about a conversation I had with someone, my memories start with an image of that person and the place where we were talking, not the words or phrases we shared, the ideas at play, however interesting our conversation might have been.

"Have any of your films started with a specific image?"

What sometimes invites me to explore a story, what acts most strongly on my decision to make a film, is an image within which the entire conception of the film is somehow contained. *The Wedding Suit* is based on an image I had in mind, of a boy watering geraniums in the early morning. *Where is the Friend's House?* was inspired by the image of a child running towards a tree at the end of a road that threads its way into a barren hillside. I had been thinking about that one for years. You can see it in my paintings and the photos I was taking at the time. It was as if I were being unconsciously pulled towards this hill with its solitary tree, which I faithfully reconstructed on film. With *Where is the Friend's House?* I rediscovered images of long ago: a street, a dog, a child, an old man, all of which were elements of *Bread and Alley*, my first film. They came flooding back years later. The dogs that scared me as a child are lurking somewhere in my unconscious. Given the opportunity, those experiences won't hesitate to burst forth and haunt me. The idea for *Like Someone in Love* was triggered nearly twenty years before I made the film. I was in Tokyo, driving through town late one night, and saw a young girl dressed in a white bridal gown, standing on the pavement, surrounded by businessmen in dark suits carrying briefcases. If I had taken a photograph of this scene perhaps I would never have made the film, but because that photo doesn't exist I was able to play with the image in my head over the years, steadily adjusting and adapting it, until finally it accommodated other ideas of mine.

"In the beginning was the word." But consider who spoke that word. What was he wearing? What colour were her eyes? Things might have started with a word, but where did this utterance take place? On whose estate was he standing? In olden days, you had to write scripts to prove you were a filmmaker and because producers needed certain guarantees, but today, because everything is so much cheaper, I don't see the need to write anything down. We can prove ourselves with the films themselves. At the heart of Persian culture lies the written word, and there can be no doubt that reading and writing will educate your instincts. But why shouldn't filmmakers start directly with the image? Thought, feeling and expression without words is not just possible. It is encouraged.

※ ※ ※

I had something in mind for the final shot of *Through the Olive Trees* and searched high and low for the right landscape. When I found it, I went back several times to determine what time of day had the most interesting light, which turned out to be just before sundown. The idea was to film from far away so we would see Tahereh in the distance, slowly departing, with Hossein chasing after her. The insurmountable class barrier between them means that Tahereh can never agree to marry Hossein, all the more so because her parents – when they were alive – had already rejected him. The dead exert a strong influence in Iran. When someone says something before departing, their decisions are set in stone.

During rehearsals, I watched the two of them walking away, disappearing from view, like two patches of white merging together. We stayed there for twenty days, waiting for the perfect moment, for the most beautiful light, which lasted only four minutes each day. For nearly three weeks I looked at that superb countryside. It was almost like going into a meditative trance, as if the image before me went hand-in-hand with an incantation. Away from the city, from codified social differences, the scene takes place within a dreamland that knows no boundaries. As the camera rolled, all real-world problems dropped away. I dipped into reveries myself, hoping Tahereh might at last give Hossein a positive answer. It was a perfect opportunity to break free from the anchor of reality and, for a moment, follow the path of imagination.

❀ ❀ ❀

I like the idea of making a film with no credits, where no single person has a claim to being the driving force. A compromise would be to present audiences with a straightforward list of names at the end of the film, without specifying who did what.

❀ ❀ ❀

Self-confidence is vital. But self-importance is unappealing, the most unpleasant of traits. Humility pays dividends.

❀ ❀ ❀

Poetry should be read uninflected, like a newsreader. Let the words themselves express meaning.

❀ ❀ ❀

Kiarostami sits with a handful of participants in his hotel lobby.

You can't enter the world of cinema exclusively via literature and poetry, through the realm of the word. Appreciation and understanding of the image is vital. As a filmmaker, only by looking closely at the world and then creating your own images can you arrive at your own definition of beauty. If a photographer wants to consider the evolution of his aesthetic sensitivity, of his feelings and tastes, he puts his prints up on the wall and studies them. I make a film every two years, but rarely a day passes when I don't take a photo.

At every minute the world bombards us with a never-ending mosaic of compositions and forms. Photography is a way of helping us differentiate exceptional images from lesser ones. In every one of us are two glistening jewels – our eyes – of inestimable value that should be cherished. What photography

116

does is train us to use them. It illuminates by teaching us to see, to develop the requisite skills, to decide which are the most balanced and harmonious images and which we should discard. It allows us to store up images in our mind that we can draw upon.

When asked how long I have been interested in photography, I say it began around the time I started taking an interest in nature. The value of film lies in its ability to show the leaves of a tree moving in the wind. But photography freezes one particular, ephemeral moment and immortalises it in a mysterious way that cinema isn't able to. Photography for me doesn't involve just pushing a button and capturing a static image. It's about leaving town and heading into nature, braving and embracing piercing winds, enduring blinding, burning sunshine, submerging into pure white snow, standing absolutely still and listening to the darkness, experiencing the flow of moonlight and gazing at the stars, roaming freely and becoming wholly engulfed. All this while waiting patiently for the moment. It's a form of meditation, like the anticipation felt by a fisherman awaiting his catch. The number of fish he brings back is unimportant.

I am sometimes forced to take photos of friends, but rarely show them to anyone. I took photos of people in Africa, but there was such a connection between them and their environment that I don't feel I betrayed my favourite subject. When you love someone you take her picture and add it to the family album. Photographing landscapes is my way of sharing beauty with people who aren't able to witness the marvels of such things for themselves. Those images are a glorious gift I can give, these views of the garden, of the desert. It would be a form of torture not to be able to take photographs in nature and show them to people.

My years of photography – of taking refuge outdoors – have taught me much about myself and my true feelings about the world. When I look at a tree in one of my photographs, it can seem happy and healthy or lonely and sad. Sometimes I get the feeling that trees understand something about me that most human beings don't. Ibn Arabi wrote that the tree is the sister of man. When I look at photos I took, years apart, of the same set of trees, it's as if I am staring at a fading photograph of my classmates from school. This one died years ago, this one is a famous doctor who hasn't been in touch for years, this one has been twice married and divorced, this one is forever busy with his family, this one vanished from his circle of friends years ago. Who doesn't appreciate trees? Their value is incalculable. They stand upright, perfectly placed in the landscape, their powerful trunks protecting us. We lie in their shadows when the sun is high. We eat the fruit they bear and use their wood for a multitude of purposes. We breathe the air they create. We are buried at their feet. They are truly admirable creatures. Sohrab wrote of the elm offering its branches to the crows for free, but never selling its shadow to the highest bidder. I remember in London being intrigued by the fact that I could walk into a museum for free, but had to pay to enter the local botanic gardens.

"Did you ever study photography?"

I am self-taught. Political events in 1979 slowed our work as filmmakers, so I bought a camera and escaped. The city – noise, people, turbulence, the enclosed spaces and artificial light – weighs heavily on me and has become ever more difficult to endure. At the same time, I have discovered the sheer pleasure of being surrounded by nature, in all its bewitching, magnetic glory. Sky, trees, water. Such things are a sort of sedative for me, an emancipation, an incitement to dream. A retreat from the disunity and sterility of the city animates and strengthens. It provides me with boundless energy. Rigidity drops away and rejuvenation takes place. The deadening of senses is exacerbated by city life, while the garden refreshes. It purifies and nourishes, helping me defragment. The pain of isolation, of being misunderstood by those closest to me, of those things that can overwhelm in the city, all evaporate in the countryside. There, I am an undiscovered person. The wilderness is a balm that allows me to unburden myself. The important thing is being able to penetrate the open space, to experience the running streams, mountain slopes, flowered glades and thick forests, all of which happens to be accompanied by the act of picking up a camera.

Take a look at how many films I have made in rural areas. Stories set outside cities, away from urban living, are easier to get past the censor in Iran. But there is another more important reason. Nature might not mean anything to someone born in an apartment and happy with city living, but I doubt it, because that would be contrary to human nature. Paradise is never imagined as buildings, traffic jams, pollution, crowds and billboards. The road I took to school every day was surrounded by fields. The image of golden corn blowing in the wind, the sound of chirping beetles, are all forever in my mind. Every day, working on *The Wind Will*

Carry Us, once we had finished filming, I would go into the fields and feel drunk, as if rediscovering sensations and a physical space I had removed myself from years ago. Rumi writes that those who are separated from their origins, those estranged from their essence, energetically seek union with such things.

There is little permanence in life. Attachment drops away as we get older. Desire dissipates. The attraction of everything diminishes. The longing for things I once considered important – friends, family, food, possessions – evaporates. I don't have the same degree of worry about my children as I used to. My appetite for good food and the company of others isn't what it was. I feel comfortable leaving it all behind. What has taken the place of all this, and is becoming ever stronger as each day passes – something I never found interesting when younger, never understood – is a desire to detach from the ostentation of cities, to build a union with the outside world, to examine the bewildering, resounding immensity of the sky overhead, to experience the changing of the seasons, those moments when nature reveals itself to us anew. The thought of being unable to enjoy this is the only thing that makes me fear death. If we could bring nature with us, mortality would lose all meaning.

I used to paint, but never called myself a painter. I couldn't accept the end product of my time in front of a canvas as a work of art, only a painting I had done, one lingering on details that were apparently insignificant for everyone else. I would look at the world but could never bring myself to paint it. I would create landscapes in a hyperrealist style, though I have always known that the camera does it better. Nature will always be a more effective painter, capable of depicting the world in all its complexity. The photographic representation of nature is incomparable. Sometimes a shutter click – a fraction of a second – is all it takes to capture a moment and make it eternal, while it might take me twenty hours to complete a simple drawing or painting of a landscape. My illustrations have no inherent value, but those twenty hours are precious to me.

Concentrating on a single point, lingering on details that are probably insignificant to everyone else, helps create order in my mind. It's meditation more than anything else. At my age, photography has replaced painting for me. I prefer the mechanical recording of nature's wonders, which my paintbrush could never compete with. Sometimes I leave home at one in the morning and drive for hours to reach a spot outside town, where I can capture a particular image, like the rising sun, which I wait patiently and joyously for. It's only when you are alone, face-to-face with nature – with yourself – that the strange purity of photography comes to light. Not even the click of the shutter, as it captures the moment, can break the silence. I sometimes tell myself I should devote myself entirely to photography.

"Do you shoot film or digital?"

These days only digital.

"When you did shoot on film, did you print your own photos?"

Always. I took my time in the darkness, as if trying to prolong the moment of tranquillity. It was an important part of the process. For me, a photograph has value only if it isn't modified at the moment of printing. I create the image I want at the moment of capture. That's why the white frame around a photograph has to be visible if it is to retain its value, as proof that there have been no adjustments. The perspective of the photographer when in natural surroundings is what's important, not the result of choices made in the darkroom, as he removes what he isn't happy with. When I work with framers at galleries, sometimes they adjust the photo so that a couple of millimetres are missing, out of sight. "It's nothing to be concerned about," they tell me. But I know something important is missing.

❀ ❀ ❀

A moving image doesn't permit as much freedom of thought and participation as a well-crafted static image. The photograph of a road leading to the unseen opens up an unknown world to us. We see footsteps in snow and our imagination is sparked. We are provoked into thought. An entire story pulls itself together in our mind. A photo is never the whole story.

❀ ❀ ❀

Some poetry makes me sleepless. At night, when I read certain poems, when the window of my bedroom is dark, I hear the songs of sparrows.

❀ ❀ ❀

Horizontal images feel more natural to me, so I prefer taking photos horizontally. After all, our eyes are set in a horizontal fashion. Sometimes I wish I had been born with rectangular bars attached to my pupils so that the sacred frame would be with me at all times. And I try to avoid a God's eye view. Photographing things from ground level – from a human viewpoint, from one's own side of the kitchen table to the other – is best.

❀ ❀ ❀

I communicate with participants at these workshops not unlike the way I interact with actors on set. I don't give instructions. At least, none that I expect anyone to heed without question. All I do is create the right conditions and atmosphere, then let everyone loose.

❀ ❀ ❀

Don't fret if one of your ideas doesn't work. Find another concept within which you can explore that idea. Or just find another idea.

❀ ❀ ❀

In nature, when communicating with God, half the usual problems of misinterpretation between two people vanish.

❀ ❀ ❀

We made *The Choir* in Rasht, a couple of hundred miles from Tehran, and when filming was over, most of the crew quickly returned home. I was left by myself to walk those narrow streets with their old wooden doorways and cement and plaster walls, covered in moss. I stayed for several days, passing time taking photographs, in perfect harmony, without having to involve myself in discussions with the cameraman, sound engineer and crew. For weeks I had been constrained by the script, having to deal with all the problems inherent to a film shoot. But now I could look, in perfect freedom, free from all interference, for the images I wanted, and just contemplate.

❀ ❀ ❀

It is one of the characteristics of art that forms can and must be renewed, and by so doing, advanced. The reinvention of the ancient is always acceptable. And, at times, necessary.

❀ ❀ ❀

I once had an assistant who lived with me. He married and brought his wife to live with him. She didn't leave the house for an entire year because she found the noises and crowds of the city so oppressive. Eventually, I forced her husband to take her outside for a stroll around the neighbourhood. "Did you enjoy it?" I asked her, on their return. "No," she said. "It hurt my face."

❀ ❀ ❀

Nature isn't an easy lover. She will always overcome us, but at the same time she calms. Stillness. Quiet. And yet restlessness, but in a way wholly different to that experienced in the city. Time spent in nature is a sort of sacrament. Today, solitude is more important to me than ever. I find myself battling what the city offers, and in this respect nature – free of people – has become a powerful ally. My heart is fixed on the open air. When you realise how insignificant we are before the grandeur of nature, that we are entitled to nothing, expectations decrease. One's outlook is transformed. A yearning for self-improvement evaporates.

❀ ❀ ❀

Walk until you are bent, holding your knees, listening to each breath. Then sit and read a book of poetry. Reflect on life, on your place in the world. Shed your frustrations. Just enjoy.

❀ ❀ ❀

I have been suffering from toothache all week, so yesterday went to the dentist. I was stuck in traffic and arrived late, but thankfully she and her assistant were still there. She was actually with another patient. I was in the waiting room, pacing up and down, in pain, when I heard the most beautiful flute music coming from her room, and stopped dead in my tracks. Then the music stopped and a well-dressed gentleman left her room, carrying a black box under his arm, tipping his hat my way as he left. The dentist appeared and beckoned me into her room. "Who was that man?" I asked. "A professional flautist who needed a tooth filed down," she said. "It was getting in the way of his playing."

※ ※ ※

There is an optimal number of words needed to tell a story. It is almost always the smallest number.

※ ※ ※

Post-production on *The Wind Will Carry Us* took nine months. The sound editor and I didn't see eye-to-eye, so he left without finishing the job. After four or five months of stasis, the film seemed to die. I had distanced myself from it so radically, and suppressed certain unhappy experiences during production, that I didn't want anything to do with it. If I hadn't been contractually obliged to deliver the completed film to the producer, I might never have finished the editing myself. Eventually, fortunately, little by little, I became reconciled with *The Wind Will Carry Us*. It was a useful lesson for me. If production on a film takes too long, its creator runs the risk of losing interest. There is an incessant stream of other ideas – fresher, more interesting – banging on the door. Always finish what you start. And quickly. What's that expression? Familiarity breeds contempt.

※ ※ ※

Philosophers and prophets tend to prescribe, but people naturally resist that sort of instruction. Who wants to be preached at and humiliated? Poets have a more delicate and indirect approach. They merely suggest how we might tackle life, how others have done so before us. The best film is a parable, which is a more gentle, subtle form of teaching. And of protest.

※ ※ ※

A film featuring people doing things that don't exist in the real world – unreal things – is of little interest to me. My films show real people, real characters, real personalities. It's the same with my poems, in which I try to reflect the world as it truly is, as if I were taking a photograph of a flower. Poetry for me is the translation of real life into words and images.

❀ ❀ ❀

Don't burrow too deep inside your ideas and theories. Just present them to us, as unformed as they might be. Let images do their work.

❀ ❀ ❀

Being realistic isn't necessarily a worthwhile aspiration. Being truthful is. An audience's interest doesn't dissolve if it considers something unreal, only if it finds something unbelievable. Exploring reality is the best way to achieve truthfulness.

❀ ❀ ❀

An idea for a film that comes from Kuleshov. At least, I think it's Kuleshov. A man, sitting on a park bench, who from time to time looks up. We see what he sees: a child playing and her mother giving her a hug. Cut back to the man. The child falls to the ground and starts crying. Cut back to the man. A funeral procession moves through the park. Cut back to the man. His first reaction to the child and mother is one of compassion and affection, the second is concern, the third sadness. The point, as I'm sure you all know, is that the three images of the man reading the newspaper are exactly the same. The audience of a film cannot help but project its feelings and interpretations. A single image pulls in meaning from everything around it.

❀ ❀ ❀

An Iranian tale of goats grazing outside a studio. The producers inside decide to adapt a book into a film and give the goats a copy of the book to graze on. The film is a flop, so the producers throw the reels out. "The book tasted better," say the goats.

A conversation overheard, between two workshop participants.

"I was with the group that Abbas took to the museum around the corner. I was standing, watching the glass elevator as it went up and down, and decided to film it. When I had finished, Abbas asked to look at the footage. He stood there, watching the screen on my camera, then said, 'I want you to come back to this spot tomorrow with three actors and a camera. Create a scene between them that follows an elevator journey but remains unresolved by the time they reach the bottom.' I made the mistake of saying that I hoped I could get permission to film there. 'Permission? What are you talking about?' he said, then walked away."

"Did you go back to the museum the next day?"

"I didn't dare not go after that, though I couldn't find anyone to be in the film, so ended up shooting a lot of footage and cutting the material into an experimental montage."

"Did you show it to Abbas?"

"He saw me editing and asked me if I had found anything specific to film. 'Not really,' I told him. 'The end result is basically one big abstraction.' He threw his arms in the air and said, 'Another abstraction! Everyone here is making abstract films!' He shook his head and walked away. What about your idea?"

"The first one I pitched in class was embarrassingly bad, but I just wanted to get started. I came up with a half-baked idea of shooting a lift with a camera that's been tilted ninety degrees, so that up would be camera left and down would be camera right. Abbas asked me what that would add. He said it was just a conceptual gimmick. By the way, I overheard Abbas's interpreter talking on the telephone earlier. He said that from the start he has been toning down comments, that Abbas has been more dismissive of our ideas than we will ever know. 'This is an unworkable idea' becomes 'You might want to give it more thought.'"

Every film needs internal logic, some sort of theme, a satisfying and unifying element, an idea the audience can take away and mull over. Without that, however coherent your images and scenes, they will be unbound and disunified. However graceful a poem is, if it has no application to my life – some potential effect – I lose interest. A beautiful poem is even more beautiful when it has meaning. Form for its own sake goes only so far. I long to be useful.

❀ ❀ ❀

I never consciously think about the form of my work because form derives from content. Or better, the two permeate each other. You can never separate them. One leads directly to the other. Form is dictated by content. Consider the differences between 35mm and digital. The choice between the two isn't predetermined, it depends on the story being told. Once the story is in place, once it is inhabited by characters, the decision about how to represent things on screen – the medium of expression, the form – flows naturally. And if the form of a piece of art is interesting enough, if it is original and innovative, its creator doesn't even need to think about content. The content is the form.

❀ ❀ ❀

Ubiquity is no indication of quality. Look beyond what they hand you at the multiplex. There is much more to explore. Don't allow someone else to set the parameters, to dictate the conversation. Accept nothing without questioning. Create your own apparatus. Dig away and find the riches. They are almost never on the surface.

❀ ❀ ❀

New ideas need to be absorbed, not resisted. Filmmaking is a continuous evolution, an unbroken education. But I confess that at my age, I register little novelty. I can understand why some people are always wearing headphones, feeding themselves music, but I have no need for that. There is already too much going on in my head, including music, without me sending in more. I filled my head with so many images and stories as a young man that I have been drawing on them ever since. I haven't been able to get through even a fraction of this mass. Within my immediate grasp is enough material to last a dozen lifetimes. The truth is that these days I find myself recording very few events around me. You, who are all much younger, have no such excuse.

❈ ❈ ❈

I don't understand what you are saying to me. Tell me again, slower, in twenty words or less. And don't mumble.

❈ ❈ ❈

Day five.

Most participants are editing their films in the basement. Kiarostami is in conversation with Natia, a radiant, curly-haired young journalist from Georgia who is writing an article about the workshop.

My films have become lighter in tone over the years. As time passes, perhaps I have less courage to confront heavy subjects, in the same way that my back doesn't permit me to carry heavy loads.

"Yesterday you told me that an essential condition of an artist is solitude."

Yes, but the notion of solitude doesn't necessarily have negative connotations.

"Are you lonely?"

I might be alone, but I'm not aching with loneliness. Sharing joy with someone can be glorious, but these days being by myself isn't so bad. I can walk faster down the street. When I talk about being alone, I don't necessarily mean being without a partner. It's more a state of mind. One of my poems goes something like, "The moon is alone, the sun is alone, man is alone, woman is alone, couples are alone." Love gives sustenance. It can revive and speed everything up. It can be beautiful, even intoxicating. Perhaps the true value of loving someone is that it permits the abandonment of self. But love also carries with it a destructive force. Passion – the beloved – means suffering. We reach our destination sooner, but there are more possibilities of being pulled off-course. It's like the steroids that athletes use. Once they boost themselves up, there is a greater distance to fall.

There are agonies involved in surrendering oneself. Brief happiness can be followed by long-lasting sorrow. They say that when a man and a woman are attracted to each other, holding each other's hands, it's like two wrestlers shaking hands before a fight. You accept the inevitable confrontations, then enjoy the adventure of love. As for me, I am neither disappointed in love, nor have I lost hope. Age has taught me to be honest and realistic about such things. As we get older, cautiousness takes over and courage diminishes. It was a different story when I was younger. Love in the time of youth is an exceptional thing. They say that if you don't have the guts of a lion, don't run after love.

Kiarostami looks into the wide eyes of his interviewer and points to her hand.

I notice you wear a gold ring on that particular finger, so I wonder if you are still ready to run, if you still allow yourself to be empowered by the extraordinary potential of love. Hafez says that our faith in God can be shaken by a beautiful woman. Have you read Omar Khayyám's poetry? I adore his intelligence and sensuality, his brevity and precision. Reading his beautiful work is like being slapped in the face. It's a continuous elegy to life in the omnipresence of death, pushing us to consider the human condition at all times. According to Khayyám, life passes by so quickly that every second counts. Our aim should be one pleasurable moment after another, to live life to the full. We mustn't forgo even an instant when we might enjoy ourselves. This is why Khayyám praises wine and the drunken joyousness that accompanies it.

At the same time, has anyone experienced love without paying a price? True joy comes only from a broken heart and having lived through suffering, from the experience of pain. True happiness will never be found in a discotheque. Khayyám lets us know that we aren't able to appreciate life until we have confronted death and learned to co-exist with it. His poems place us unceremoniously but optimistically in confrontation with our mortality.

❖ ❖ ❖

I consider being married for more than a decade, then making a clean break, an achievement.

❖ ❖ ❖

The love that Rumi writes about – the kind that burns within, that seizes hold, that involves absolute acceptance, that creates a painful connection to the beloved, rendering us helpless, ushering us down a road of suffering and sacrifice – is different from the blissful, romantic love that exists between two people. Romantic love lacks the mystical qualities of Rumi's divine and unfathomable love, of his absolute devotion to the unknown, compared to which other kinds of love are cold, vulgar and powerless. For Rumi, just the fact that the beloved can create in us the desire to experience love, the capacity for love, the sensation of wanting to love, of generosity and giving, of longing, is enough. His notion of love doesn't require another person, only an acknowledgement of the world around us, and our surrender to it.

❖ ❖ ❖

Every time an artist makes something, during the act of creation, he lives and dies. During production of a film, the anxiety and chronic insomnia I experience – the nightmares and self-doubt, the fear of failure, the shockwaves of scepticism – can be crippling. But by the end of it, upon completion, whatever the result, I am born again, able to start afresh. Most people live only a single life, but an artist lives many. Every work of art is an all-consuming gift. It takes everything from its creator, but ultimately gives life. The wondrous thing is that I can live over and over again as I experience each new project, as new things unveil themselves to me. Art drains, but it also renews and prolongs life. Each new opportunity to create is a chance to become whole again, for rebirth.

❀ ❀ ❀

Talking about my work isn't easy for me. It's not that I'm unwilling to do so, but that I feel incapable. Once completed, a project – its meaning, the reasons why I did it – quickly drop away. And why shouldn't they? Always comes the next project. Being surrounded by journalists is oppressive, like being a nail hit by a hammer, in part because they always seem to ask the kinds of questions expected of psychoanalysts. I am also certain that little of what I say is worth being heard. Having to answer questions about my films is the punishment I endure each time one is completed and revealed to the world. The souls of filmmakers are fragile. The age of the interview has long been upon us, but it has never made me happy to comply. Too much like the lamb lying down with the lion.

❀ ❀ ❀

There are few enough advantages to old age, but one is that we are liberated from certain stifling rules and commitments. If death is nearer, what punishment for deviation and bluntness could possibly have meaning?

❀ ❀ ❀

Too many films have a constantly shifting viewpoint. When filming a scene, fixed camera angles – and only a limited number of them – are preferable. For the past few days, I have been sitting here, on this chair, in this corner of the room, which is the equivalent of a single camera, a single angle, a single point of view. We see and hear each other. We understand each other. There is no need for one of us to move.

❀ ❀ ❀

Years ago I saw Ingmar Bergman's film *Scenes from a Marriage*. I don't understand a word of Swedish and the print had no subtitles. When I came out of the cinema, I bought another ticket for the film and watched it again. Years later, the translated screenplay was published. After reading it, I realised that what I had guessed about the couple in the story was very different to the tale Bergman was actually telling. I enjoyed my version better.

❀ ❀ ❀

Footballers play better at home even though the rules of the game are the same everywhere. When you take a tree that is rooted in the ground and transfer it from one place to another, the fruit it bears will likely not be so tasty. My best work is probably the work I do at home.

❀ ❀ ❀

While making *Bread and Alley*, my first film, I was sure people wouldn't like it, so I kept adding music, thinking that would keep everyone entertained. It took time for me to realise that my films don't need music, or at least not as much as most others. I am the kind of filmmaker who gives a great deal of thought to every detail – including the slightest sound effect – so it isn't easy for me to have someone write an entire score for one of my films. I once commissioned music from a young composer who gave me seventeen minutes of good material, but I struggled to incorporate it into the film I was making. Hoping his work would fit the images I had created was like an arranged marriage, as if the front door swung open and my mail-order bride were standing there.

Music is a stimulating form of art that carries with it tremendous emotional charge. It can – with a single beat – excite or calm. It can make audiences steadily happy or sad, or immediately confuse and infuriate them. I would rather my images not have to compete with music, which is one of the most conscious and significant impositions a director can make. It's as if he were standing next to the screen like a conductor, waving his hands, demanding that we show our feelings, telling us from moment to moment that now is the time to be concerned or frightened or relieved. I have faith in the images in my films, and don't feel they need to be so reinforced. I want viewers to be restless on their own terms, in control of what they take in, able to make up their own minds. Whipping up emotions is too much like picking pockets in the dark, manipulating for my own ends, pushing a pre-packaged film on an audience. That intimidation will continue for as long as technology and special effects, rather than the creative mind of the filmmaker – the human soul – is the driving force of cinema. How overloaded with information can an audience be before it kicks back?

Think about an intricate tracking shot that makes you wonder how the camera got from the courtyard through the window and into the bedroom. You are following the magic of the camera instead of the story.

I am – and always have been – a rather restless and impatient person. At a young age, I became convinced that the root of all art lies in curiosity, that nothing is predetermined or pre-established. As a child I was rather timid, rarely speaking to anyone, and wasn't a particularly good pupil at school, which I compensated for by painting. During class, I would often be drawing with my coloured pencils. For me, it was therapy more than anything else, as if I were searching for a natural truth in the world of colours. Drawing relaxed me, and nowadays, when I walk in nature with a camera, I experience the same sensation.

The first things children ask when they learn to speak is "Why? Who? What?" Most people stop asking those questions as they get older, but I never did. I would endlessly seek answers. The days are hot in Iran, and as a child, during our afternoon nap, I never felt like sleeping, so became a nuisance to anyone who did. I was always in search of something to do, and ended up bothering the grown-ups while they were trying to relax. I would go out onto the balcony and draw, or head down to the basement, put two pieces of wood together, and hammer in a nail. I still feel the need to keep busy. I am unable to live a day without having something to work on. When I frame a photograph I have taken and hang it on the wall, it doesn't take long for me to turn my back on it and focus on something else. At a certain point, a realisation comes that there isn't much time left, that you have to compulsively empty yourself as quickly and efficiently as possible of everything still inside. If I get up in the morning and have nothing urgent to divert me, I can't function. When I am unable go out filming because it's Friday night and everyone is out having fun, and will be busy all weekend, and there is nobody around to work with, and I don't have the energy to drive out of town, from the garret into the glorious forest, so I can take photographs, I feel useless. That's when I pick up a book of poetry or scribble down some of my own verse or take care of the house or paint or carve a piece of wood or organise my photos for an exhibition. I have to be doing something useful.

All this activity is about finding a way to communicate, about discovering new challenges, about expressing myself, about alleviating my occasional sense of despondency, about ridding myself of whatever is lurking in the back of my mind. I don't think I have ever found an activity that truly satisfies. Carpentry probably comes closest.

You cannot create true art with a hidden camera.

If it weren't able to record the subtleties and variations of the human face, cinema would be incapable of depicting the solitude and beauty of man.

Why did you film the actors standing in front of a wall? Open up the shot. Use the physical space around them. Frame someone within his environment and learn how such things can contribute to the story. The only reason you should ever place performers up against a wall is if you intend to have them executed.

❀ ❀ ❀

The accumulation of experiences – the paths I have taken, then abandoned – has made me who I am today. I broke with my family at the age of eighteen and was obliged to earn a living. I had no intention of becoming a filmmaker. Everything happened by chance. Being confronted by those blank canvases at art school was a definitive moment for me, and pushed me to start experimenting with graphic design, photography and woodcarving. It took me thirteen years to complete a four-year degree because I held onto my day job. After graduation, I worked as a painter and graphic artist, designing book jackets and posters. My job was to squeeze the entire story of a film into a single image for the poster. This art of radical compression is achieved through simplicity and elegance. Just like a poem.

One day, I went to the biggest company in town that produced commercials and presented myself as a director. They asked me to write a sketch about a water heater, so overnight I composed a poem. I pictured a wintry setting, the first snowfall, those cold and snowy streets, and people inside a house huddled around a heater. A few weeks later I was watching television and – to my surprise – saw a commercial featuring my poem. They even paid me for it. That was the start of my career as a filmmaker. I progressed little by little, writing sketches, and eventually, over a period of years, made about one hundred and fifty commercials.

When I earned a living as a graphic artist and was making commercials, my job was to convey everything to audiences in the limited space of a single magazine page or minute-long film. It's a skilful enterprise because the weaknesses of a short film – which is what a commercial is – are not easily compensated for. Every element needs to be carefully thought out. Not a single frame can be wasted. You have to engage the audience immediately and prepare it for a message, give it that message, make sure the message has been understood, then bring everything to some sort of conclusion, all in only sixty seconds. A beginning, middle and end. A targeted audience has to be persuaded to buy a product. An advertisement for a bank has to be so good that anyone who sees it immediately drops whatever he is doing and runs out to open an account. I was told that while my films were good, they weren't good enough when it came to selling things.

When creating a static image, a great deal of thought goes into designing a column layout or the frame of a page, so the reader is immediately drawn into the limited space. The eyes are carefully guided from top to bottom and side to side. Making commercials and designing titles was my film school. I learned to condense as effectively as possible and evoke the subject by creating something universally comprehensible, all with a minimum of means, all while working under a maximum of constraints. Restrictions, as usual, served as a challenge.

❀ ❀ ❀

The first film I ever saw was a strip of celluloid I held in my hands. In Tehran, when I was young, there were stores that sold film by the foot. My school friends and I bought lots of single frames that we held up against the light and studied, though I had no idea who all these people were. One was of a man who had a moustache, neatly combed hair and a big smile. Years later, I realised it was Clark Gable. We would collect these fragments like stamps, sticking them into albums and swapping them between ourselves. We kept the close-ups of women, of course, all these dreamlike characters whose names we didn't know. We also discovered that nitrate film stock was extremely flammable, so we invented a game for ourselves by setting fire to these scraps and watching them shoot into the air.

"Was your family artistic?"

I don't remember anything remotely cultural going on in the home where I grew up. There was nothing specific in my environment that might have pushed me towards a career in cinema.

"There was no burning desire to become a film director?"

Filmmaking for me began with needing a job. It's as simple as that. In 1969, the director of the Institute for the Intellectual Development of Children and Young Adults in Tehran, who also owned an advertising firm, saw one of my films about a frying pan. He wanted to start a filmmaking department and invited me to collaborate. It was a lucrative job and at the time I was married, so I accepted his offer. If I had started working at a place that made documentaries, I would have been a documentary filmmaker. As it was, I quickly became accustomed to the easy conditions of filmmaking at the Institute because I never had to search for a producer. Initially, I was the only filmmaker there, and my first film, *Bread and Alley*, was the first production of the filmmaking department. There were eventually six or seven of us making films there, but after 1979 all my co-workers left for Europe or the United States. I was alone once again.

"Did you see many films as a child?"

I had more of a taste for cinema than my friends, who are now businessmen, doctors and painters. I liked cinema as entertainment, and rarely went to see a film because of its director. Vittorio De Sica's films particularly excited me, though it goes without saying that Sophia Loren meant more to me than anything. She filled my adolescent universe like nobody else could. Her beauty outshone everything.

"What about American cinema?"

I watched American films because they were so different from what Iranian filmmakers were doing. They have always been full of characters – those cowboys and gangsters shooting away – far removed from the lives of most of us and I had fun watching those fantasies being played out. But it was Italian neorealism that really got under my skin because that was the first time I saw people – those onscreen characters – who were so similar to the ordinary folks I spent time with every day. It was an uncannily familiar world to me. Compared to Italian films, American cinema was alien to our lives in Iran. After discovering Italian cinema, I remember thinking that my neighbour could be the hero of a film. Iranian culture is somehow similar to that of Italy, which is probably one reason why neorealism had a strong effect on me.

I once won an award named after Roberto Rossellini, and was asked by a journalist if I saw any similarities between my work and Rossellini's, and which of his films I liked the most. I couldn't think of a single one. The truth is that I don't feel I belong to any well-defined school of cinema. Imitation doesn't interest me, and I have never understood what one artist can do for another, apart from sharing a conversation and a cup of coffee every now and then. If there are similarities between my films and

Rossellini's – and perhaps that trio of Dreyer, Bresson and Ozu – they have nothing to do with the formal qualities of my work. It's simply that we look at life with the same tilt of the head.

"Are there any directors whose work you particularly appreciate?"

I leave that question for others to answer. Many of my interests and tastes are transient, always changing, so when I tell you about certain films or directors I like, I am telling you more about me than the work in question. It's been years since I was an enthusiastic cinemagoer. I see very few films these days. Apart from a brief period many years ago when I spent time in Prague, I probably haven't seen more than fifty films my whole life, and couldn't claim that any one filmmaker has been a strong influence on my work. There are no more than twenty sequences in the history of cinema that I find truly significant.

Years ago, while brushing my teeth one night, from inside the bathroom of my hotel room, I noticed Fellini's *La Strada* playing on television. Transfixed, I stood there and watched the whole thing. A few years later, I emerged from a screening of *La Dolce Vita* and could do nothing other than walk the darkened streets, deep in thought. I have never forgotten those final images, of the seashore and the hope they contained and concealed. I was interested in Godard for a time, though he never directly influenced my work, and for a couple of days considered Hitchcock a master, though today I find his films too artificial and fabricated. I can appreciate how technically accomplished his work is, but such things no longer impress me. When I began making films, I stopped going to the cinema so I wouldn't be weighed down by references. Film is first and foremost a personal quest. A few years ago, I attempted a reconciliation with filmgoing, but nothing came of it. I don't have the time or energy to invest in watching a film when chances are it isn't going to be of much interest to me.

❀❀❀

Watch a film with your heart and you will be more forgiving than if you watch it with your head.

❀❀❀

My mind is like a laboratory or refinery, with ideas as crude oil. It's as if there were a filter channelling the assorted suggestions in different directions. An image comes to mind and ends up imposing itself so obsessively that I find no rest until something is done with it, until it is somehow incorporated into a project. This is where poetry proves itself to be so convenient and useful for me. Some of the images in my head are simple, like someone drinking wine from a disposable cup, a box of wet matches in an abandoned house, a broken stool sitting in my back yard. But others are more complex, like a white foal emerging and then disappearing into the fog, a graveyard covered in snow that is melting on only three headstones, one hundred soldiers going into their barracks on a moonlit night, a grasshopper jumping and sitting, flies circling a mule as it walks from one village to the next, an autumn wind blowing leaves into my house, a child with blackened hands sitting surrounded by hundreds of fresh walnuts. How much time would it take to commit those images to film? How difficult would it be to find a subject for a film into which those images could be incorporated? This is why writing poetry is so rewarding. When I work on a poem, my desire to create an image is satisfied in only four lines. Taken together, the words become the image. My poems are like films that don't cost anything to produce. It's as if I have found a way of producing something of worth every single day. I used to take a couple of years between films, but these days rarely an hour goes by when I feel I'm not doing something useful.

Traditional poetry is rooted in the rhythm and music of words. My poems have a more imagistic quality and can be more easily transposed from one language to another without losing their meaning. They are universal. I see poetry. I don't necessarily read it.

It would be untrue to say fame has brought me freedom. I was free before, but nobody knew it.

Today, the problem isn't which project I should direct myself towards, it's that sometimes I think about doing nothing. Sitting quietly, or walking, just thinking, alone, is what I long for. Perhaps it's about waiting, though I couldn't tell you what for. Perhaps it's about recollecting past thoughts, about compiling and looking through all the images in my head. Perhaps it's about calming myself. I don't know. What I do know is that my yearning for this state of existence is, at times, overwhelming.

❀ ❀ ❀

Some call me "maestro." I can't tell you how uncomfortable that word makes me feel. I wouldn't care, except occasionally I find myself inhibited. A beginner has a world of learning and exploration ahead of him. But in which direction can a maestro move?

❀ ❀ ❀

Day six.
   Workshop participants scramble to complete their films.
   When I started work at the Institute for the Development of Children and Young Adults in Tehran, I didn't really understand children. What changed my outlook was raising two sons of my own, which became an opportunity for me to relive my own childhood. Children fascinate me. It occurs to me that we are all born as complete human beings, and only then – because society demands we not be ourselves – start acquiring defects. We emerge natural and spontaneous, then decades later die as unnatural beings. As someone once put it, we are born not as silkworms that become butterflies. We are born as butterflies, then become worms.

❀ ❀ ❀

I am the last person who should ever talk about the "themes" apparently running through my work. It isn't my mission to provide statements of intent, and I am unable to answer most questions about what my work means. My job is to ask questions, not answer them. Besides, I want everyone to have his own interpretation. When Beethoven was asked what he was trying to say with one of his sonatas, he sat down at the piano and played it

142

again. I am like a chef who is so busy preparing a dish he doesn't even know what it tastes like. The audience's interpretation is what excites me more than anything, even if it isn't what I am thinking about myself. Relish the endless ways something can be contemplated. There is no fixed meaning. Ideas about my images and films and poems shouldn't be given more credence just because I am the one who created them.

❀ ❀ ❀

I don't decide in advance that my films are going to resemble each other, but sometimes, somehow, they do. When I first told people about *Taste of Cherry*, I said it was going to be different from everything that came before it. Then, when I watched it for the first time with an audience, I realised it was very much a part of a whole, of a set of other films I had made. One journalist pointed out that the opening image of *The Wind Will Carry Us* is a more expansive version of the opening shot of my first short, *Bread and Alley*. Another one sent me an article about how balconies appear in my films and the way I always shoot them from the same angle. I had never thought about this, but it turns out he's right. The same shot appears in any number of my films. Maybe now I am aware of this I won't do it again.

Every creation is a projection of its originator, reflecting the unconscious ideas, feelings and habits of the person who made it. These creations are somehow all autobiographical acts. Perhaps we all make the same film over and over again. I conceal myself in every frame. It can't be helped.

❀ ❀ ❀

Just get on with it. The beginning is always the most difficult.

❀ ❀ ❀

Unmade projects are like books of which I have read only ten pages. They lie there with a protruding, beckoning bookmark, reminding me how much more work I have to do. One of my poems reads: "Today, like every other day, was lost for me. Half spent thinking about yesterday, half about tomorrow."

❀ ❀ ❀

Be gentle with actors. The only people who should physically move bodies around are puppeteers. There is rarely good reason to bring the camera up into the actors' faces. Keep your distance. Preserve the actor's dignity, and your own as a filmmaker.

❋ ❋ ❋

When I first watched *ABC Africa*, there was something about it I didn't like, but never bothered to change it. It can be useful for me to think about specific problems I have with my films. In fact, I enjoy watching *ABC Africa* so I can remind myself of this little mistake, correct it in my mind, and ensure it doesn't happen again. One of my poems reads: "Forgive and forget my sins. But not so that I forget them completely myself." It's appropriate that our concern with imperfection fades over time. But that doesn't mean our wrongdoings aren't occasionally useful to dwell on.

❋ ❋ ❋

Moving from place to place can help keep my mind from itself. My visits to Africa made a strong impression. Each time, I was confronted with the overwhelming need children have for love and affection. Sometimes, when I travel abroad, I shut myself up in my hotel room, feeling melancholic, and find myself wanting to eat and eat, which can be debilitating. In Africa, I experienced a powerful desire to seize hold of and bask in the vibrant life I was witness to. It is the only place outside Iran where I have ever felt an overwhelming need to take photographs.

❋ ❋ ❋

With a film made digitally, one person can be entirely responsible for the end result. That might be a definition of what we can consider art.

❋ ❋ ❋

There is a fine line between critique and complaint. Everyone appreciates the former. No one wants to be around the latter.

When one comes to know something in great detail, when one is able to make sincere and informed pronouncements about it, one generally comes to believe that the thing in question needs

145

to be changed, improved. Who comes to be so familiar with something – a location, an ideology, a piece of art, even a person – that they don't hope somehow to alter it, perhaps just a touch, perhaps quite radically, at times publicly, at times very privately?

❀ ❀ ❀

I – and my films – have long since been progressing towards a certain minimalism. I aspire to express myself in the simplest possible language, to strip things down as far as possible and remove superfluous elements. Elements that can be eliminated have been eliminated. Everything redundant is cut away. If the presence of something is of little significance, its absence is preferred.

Too much of today's cinema is comprised of the unnecessary. Do we need all that music and those establishing shots? I want to show audiences only the absolute essential. Milan Kundera said that at the end of his father's life, he spoke only two words: "How strange!" His entire vocabulary had been reduced to those two syllables. He repeated them incessantly, not because he didn't have anything else to say but because they were the most appropriate summation of his life experiences. Films of mine like *Ten* and *Five* were made with a minimum of technology and means of production. Those static cameras represent my equivalent of Mr. Kundera's two words. They sum up my existence as a filmmaker, my desire to limit the persuasive power of the director, my hope that what audiences are really absorbed in is reality, not my representation of that reality.

With *Ten*, in part because of space limitations in the car, I was able to relinquish almost all power as director and avoid unnecessary intrusions. All I did was observe and cherish because of my wonderment at how free-flowing and expressive the actors were when so unencumbered. That film might be closest to the sort of thing I expect from you this week. It was filmed entirely on video, in a single location, the *mise-en-scène* reduced to two shots, with a small – almost non-existent – crew, and non-professional actors. With *Ten*, I took one step closer to something I have been working towards for some time: the elimination of the director, the rejection of certain elements that ordinary cinema is constructed upon.

I have been steadily turning my back on the traditional job of the director, and by so doing have learned to offer actors an increasing range of possibilities, which is why so many cameramen say I spoil actors. The journey of moving towards a situation where ever more authority is given to actors, where the director can ultimately be dispensed with, is an important – and enjoyable – one for me. If I allow myself to be directed by a non-professional, rather than the other way round, the results are fascinating. The expression of the performers' real life characteristics affect audiences much more than any fictional structures I could ever bring to bear on a situation. The result is that the film director can be dispensed with almost entirely. There is a sense in which I had nothing to do with *Ten*. I just put everyone together in a car and placed all responsibility on them.

A poem by Rumi speaks of polo players and their mallets. "You are my ball, driven by the command of my mallet. I am running after you, although I guide you." Who is in control? Me or the actors? I determine the direction and supply some of the impulses and motivations, but the actors choose their own journey. Eventually they arrive at where I always planned to be, but they work out how to get there. I just follow, leading from behind. If anyone were to ask me what I did as a director on some of my films, I would say, "Nothing really. And yet without me, they wouldn't exist."

❀ ❀ ❀

At daybreak, when stray dogs wander through the streets, their emotions – the interactions between them – are clear to see. The animals communicate with each other. The third segment of *Five* is a sixteen-minute shot of waves washing up on a beach of the Caspian Sea, with the ocean and horizon in the background. I saw a group of dogs at that spot and took the trouble to put food out to see if they returned, which they did, so one morning before sunrise – while it was still dark – I took my camera and set it up on the beach, then fell asleep. When I awoke, I saw a number of dogs asleep by the water's edge. There was no input from me. All I did was create the conditions whereby something interesting might be recorded.

In *Five* is a seven-minute sequence where the principal character is a piece of wood caught in the waves. It did exactly what I wanted, moving around with such grace, giving a magnificent performance, one of the best in any of my films, breaking apart at just the right moment. I didn't direct. I just waited, dependent at all times on existing possibilities.

❀ ❀ ❀

The most important rules are self-evident and rightfully inflexible. No legal system is required to enforce them. They are real and permanent because they are true. We can't help but abide.

❀ ❀ ❀

I was once introduced to someone with the words, "This is the director of *Close-Up*," to which the other person – who wasn't involved in filmmaking – said, "I didn't think that film had a director." What a wonderful concept. An unintended compliment.

❀ ❀ ❀

The easiest – and worst – thing for a filmmaker to do is exercise too much control by telling actors what they have done wrong, by calling attention to their deficiencies. The constant, minute-by-minute presence of a director is vital when it comes to something like an animated cartoon, but with real people interference like that is unnecessary, and usually unwanted. A director who believes himself to be omnipotent creates anguish for anyone working in front of the camera, and misery for those behind it. A director who cries "Cut!" at the end of a take is liable to induce nightmares in actors. We have to bring this authoritarian deity down to earth.

❀ ❀ ❀

I argue with myself so vehemently, so constantly, that there seems little point in taking issue with the world as loudly as I sometimes want to. The internal debate keeps me busy.

❀ ❀ ❀

Making a film is like telling a joke. Some sort of punchline is needed.

❀❀❀

The way the light is coming in through that window, the shadows on the wall over there. Good to look at, and to film. Go explore

❀❀❀

Every script calls for its own working methods. Every film leaves something particular in mind. In *Taste of Cherry*, the most memorable moments are the emotions and expressions of the characters, and perhaps the tone and pace, including the silences. In *Ten*, it's probably the dialogue and distinguishing characteristics of those different personalities that makes the film worthwhile.

❀❀❀

Get beyond middle age and things calm down. Concerns drop away. One's limitations become crystal clear. Liberation dawns.

❀❀❀

Ideas we disagree with push us – sometimes gently, sometimes noisily – to respond. We grow in strength as we consider, neutralise, counteract and finally co-opt them. Enemies and obstacles can be wondrously provocative.

❀❀❀

Am I the mouthpiece for the real people in my films, or is it the other way round?

❀❀❀

It's too hot in this room. Please, open a window.

❀❀❀

Day seven.

Kiarostami screens his documentary 10 on Ten, *in which he appears, alone, talking to the camera, discussing his approach to filmmaking, while driving a car through the hills around Tehran.*

My producer suggested it as a DVD extra and I thought it was a good idea. This was a rare opportunity for me to engage in some sort of introspection and perhaps learn something about myself. There are few enough occasions in life when we make room for self-scrutiny. I started reading through old notebooks and felt that here was a chance for me to chart some of the changes in my work over the years.

"The film contains lessons on writing, music and acting. Why not one on editing?"

While some of my films were constructed in the editing room, and though some fine directors are known for relying heavily on the post-production process, the cinema I find exciting isn't so

fabricated. Editing puts great power into the hands of the filmmaker because it allows him to generate and manipulate emotion and thought in the audience. He can change what he wants, switch this person with that, replace the accused with the plaintiff, and vice versa. It was while editing a scene in *Through the Olive Trees*, where Hossein and Tahereh glance at each other – an exchange of looks that contains a shot suggesting it might actually be Tahereh who is the more amorous of the two – that I came to understand just to what extent I was able to distort things.

I consider editing to be the most artificial element of filmmaking and have never used it as a technique to patch up a film, to make certain problems less noticeable. The alterations made while editing – the re-arranging of material – can ameliorate a film but never fundamentally change it, at least not for the better. Just as through this process you can never radically improve footage of poor quality, nor will you irrevocably damage good footage. Editing will forever remain a technique, nothing more. The overall quality of the film can never be intrinsically affected by such interventions. Only during shooting can anything truly important happen. I would never say there is never a need for editing. In *Ten*, after all, the cutting enables us to move from one character to another. But my favourite sequence in that film is the opening sixteen minutes, of the boy talking to his mother, which appears to be a single shot but actually contains a few cuts, though most people don't notice them. For me, editing takes place in my head before filming. I prefer to organise reality in front of the camera rather than intervene after the fact, during editing. There is a certain creativity that manifests only during shooting.

My approach to editing is simple: I keep what I think is good and throw away everything else. Sometimes the best thing is to remove a shot, even one you have worked hard on, because it turns out to be foreign to everything around it. I might discard a moment when an actor's performance is too powerful, or a particularly interesting improvised line or interaction between characters emerges. These are the kinds of things that can distract an audience and overwhelm a film. There was a moment during the filming of *Taste of Cherry* when Ershadi began to weep. It would probably have moved some audiences, so I took out the shot. The most effective tear doesn't run down the cheek, it glistens in the eye.

"You prefer action to play out within the frame, rather than cut from shot to shot."

A match cut is one in which action in one shot continues directly in the next shot. Why do I dislike match cuts? Because they aren't realistic. We don't experience match cuts in real life. Think about the difference between the camera cutting from a shot of someone standing ten feet away to a shot of her eyes and nose and mouth, and a single, uninterrupted image of someone walking from afar towards the camera so her face fills the screen. The first is unrealistic. No one, not even the most talented cameraman, can be at two places at once.

In *Bread and Alley*, there is a static shot of an old man approaching the camera from a distance. He walks up the alley, eventually past the camera. It was the first film I had ever made, and people told me that having the character move through the frame in that way – as the immobile camera stood there – meant I clearly lacked the courage to use a tracking shot or a zoom, or find the most effective insert. I would never deny I felt nervous about continuity and crossing the line of action – all those technical things – so I accepted these criticisms because I was a newcomer. But even back then, I felt it was better to capture a scene in a single image rather than edit several shots together. Piecing images together to create a scene might result in more control over the rhythm, but the impact on audiences is deeper when things play out from a single angle. I don't think you can completely trust what you are looking at unless it's an uncut image. If I, as a director, don't believe in what is taking place in front of me, the audience won't either.

When we observe someone from a distance, waiting for him to show up, from afar, as he closes in and reveals himself, our eyes are naturally and solidly fixed on him. We notice little details. We have time to think about the way he moves, his gait, how fast he is going. Is he happy or sad? Where is he coming from? Who was the last person he spoke to? We might bring to mind all the people this person reminds us of. We also have the opportunity to explore his environment, the streets he is moving through. Daily life teaches us that we don't necessarily need to be physically close to someone in order to have an understanding of who he is. Audiences supposedly feel detached from characters faraway in the distance, but I always feel connected to such people. I like to draw back and take in the scene as a whole. I accept that cinema involves the art of editing, but some images should be left alone. They are doing everything you ask of them, so why cut? Give the audience a chance to immerse itself.

"What is the role of editing in documentary filmmaking, where footage is often collected without any pre-imposed structure?"

The job of the director and editor is to utilise their creativity and, from a mass of sounds and images, carve out a story. We are, whether we like it or not, confronted by the material we have collected. Everything that can possibly end up in your film is somewhere in that footage, in those fragments. This is all difficult enough, but what compounds the work is that oftentimes we still think idealistically about the film we set out to make all those months ago, and that in some form or another is still playing itself out in our heads. The material that lies before us never exactly corresponds to our vision of the film. The gap between that ideal and what has been achieved means only one thing: you must adapt to the reality at hand. Make a film from the footage you actually have, not from the increasingly stale idea in your mind.

We cling to the notion that there is one perfect way of putting all these shots together, that there is an optimal configuration of all this material. But alongside that one perfect shape are a multitude of workable, beautiful and interesting alternate versions that might emerge. Most filmmakers have at least a vague, preconceived idea about the sort of film they want to make before they run off with a camera. It isn't easy for a filmmaker to empty his mind while shooting and say to himself, "I will respond honestly and with no preconceptions to what is going on around me," though that's more or less what I did while making *ABC Africa*, where my camera was always a few steps ahead of me.

That film is as close to a genuine documentary as I will ever make because during shooting I didn't think it would be a film at all. I was asked if I would go to Africa and make a film about the AIDS crisis. For several years, I had been using a Hi8 camera like most people would use a pen, so when my colleague and I took our first trip to Uganda we brought along our "pens," with the idea that they would serve as sketchpads. I never considered them as serious tools. It was just visual note-taking. Our plan was to go and shoot, then find a producer and return with bigger cameras, but the rushes were so exciting that we realised there was no point in going back. There was nothing in that raw material we felt could be usefully embellished. The strength of *ABC Africa* is that we didn't impose ourselves on the footage. Our hand-held cameras turned 360 degrees, so reported an absolute truth from every angle. It was material with such stunning vitality to it – a genuine sense of exploration and investigation – something I felt could never be replicated, certainly not on film, so why return with a 35mm camera?

❀ ❀ ❀

I edit most of my own films. I am the only one who knows exactly what needs to be done with the footage, who knows which pieces need to be discarded and which need to be linked together. Besides, I enjoy being cloistered away with all that material, tasked with finding the correct way of piecing it together.

❀ ❀ ❀

Cinema wouldn't exist without editing, but cinema without editing would respect me more as a viewer. It wouldn't lie to me or lead me astray.

❀ ❀ ❀

Know when to be unswerving with your ideas, to be fixed, and when to let go of them.

❀ ❀ ❀

Take a human being, limit him to the camera frame and insist he follow a script, and you have nothing but artificiality.

❀ ❀ ❀

What happens on screen has no impact without past experiences brought by audiences. Personal recollections make the work of filmmakers that much easier. Through our work, we remind audiences of the bitterness and sweetness in their lives. Then we rush in, hold our heads up high with pride, and take credit for the powerful film we have made.

❀ ❀ ❀

The day formally ended hours ago. Kiarostami is watching a rough cut of a film and talking with the young woman who made it.

Think back to what I said on day one. You don't have to show everything. Don't underline what is already clear by implication. Whatever you can get away with not showing should be omitted. Imagine you and I are sitting in a café, chatting over a cup of coffee. We know each other, we enjoy each other's company, we are talking about something meaningful. A waiter comes over to our table and asks if we need anything. We might throw him a glance, but won't give him much attention. It isn't that we are ignoring him or being rude, but our conversation is the most crucial thing. In cinematic terms, we wouldn't give him a close-up because that would suggest he is as important to the scene as you and me, which isn't the case. Any character not an integral component of a film should be kept on the sidelines. To do otherwise means to create a state of imbalance and potentially bewilder an audience. The other side of this example is someone making a film about waiters in which there is not a single shot of customers sitting and drinking coffee in a café. Focus only on the essential.

When I watch a film and see a knife cutting someone's eye, all I can think about is how good the special effects are. Mainstream cinema shows so much that it eliminates any possibility of us imagining things for ourselves. The intended effect is undone. Watching things we shouldn't be witness to amounts to voyeurism, to pornography. I have always followed my own rule of not going where I don't have to be. The noise of water and voice of a woman singing, her shadow behind a curtain, should be enough to represent her taking a shower. By not showing certain things, by withholding, a filmmaker can more effectively trigger the audience, whose collective imagination is always richer than his own and deeper than anything that might be caught on film.

This is why I avoid point-of-view shots. If a character sees something, his reaction to what he is looking at is enough. It tells the audience everything it needs to know. We don't always have to look through a window to know what is outside. Whenever possible, I use a reaction shot or sound effect to move our attention beyond the frame, as if I am creating another film in the mind of the audience. Consequently, a single shot, in fact, can do the work of two. A film is like a deck of cards. I shuffle and deal things to viewers, each of whom arranges them in a slightly different order. There are as many interpretations of what is happening off-camera as there are members of the audience. A film that is open to different interpretations – one that facilitates a dialogue with its audience – will be more relevant than one that answers every question before sending people out into the night. I think it was Godard who said that what is on screen is already dead. Only the viewer can breathe life back into those images. A good film is an incomplete film.

"So when we don't see things in full detail, their impact is stronger?"

Almost always. My filmmaking is an invitation to the audience to participate in the creative act. Making a film is like creating a collage or doing a jigsaw puzzle. Based on my perception of things, I deliberately include certain pieces and leave others out. Each viewer makes his own unique connections between what is presented to him. I create, but I need creativity in return. The same film communicates differently to different people. I saw a fifty-year-old man storm out of a screening of *Where is the Friend's House?* insisting it was the most boring film he had ever seen. His wife was trying to calm him down. I also once met a six-year-old girl who had watched the film three times and wanted to see it again and again.

A picture hung on the wall of a hotel room I once stayed in. It showed three women – two young and one older – washing clothes beneath a beautiful sun. The scene is probably set at the beginning of the nineteenth century. All three have different looks on their faces, but all are focused in the same direction, beyond the frame of the painting. The two young women are gazing at something with admiration, while the older one is staring at the same thing with disapproval. My sense is that they are all looking at a young man. While the girls are marvelling at his appearance, the mother – while sharing her daughters' wonder – is expressing objections. She might think the man is handsome, but doesn't consider him suitable or sufficiently respectable. What these collective looks do is allow us to start constructing this man's identity. The value of a picture like this comes from its suggestive power, that we look elsewhere, not directly at the image. This is what a good film should do. When we aren't shown something, when something is excluded, when it doesn't appear through the camera lens or on the cinema screen, it's as if we see more.

It would be a crime on the part of the director if a film created a homogenous audience. I don't want to tell stories so much as have people formulate their own stories in their own minds. My films and what I present to viewers are only the starting point for people to be creative. By leaving things open, there is an endless, fathomless space for ideas to blossom. The quality of a film is defined by how deeply an audience is able to exercise its imagination. Too many films ensnare and hold us captive. They propagate a message or tell a ready-made story, then insist we react in a specific way. My films move in whichever direction the viewer wants them to.

Kiarostami screens the first twenty minutes of Shirin. *Apart from an opening overture, the film – which lasts ninety minutes – is comprised entirely of close-ups of women as they appear to respond to a visual dramatisation of the ancient Persian fable* Khosrow and Shirin *playing on the screen in front of them. We never see the film they are watching, though we hear the story and follow the reactions of the women.*

How do you make a film of a story as complex as *Khosrow and Shirin*? One way – as if peeping through a keyhole – is to show a variety of people responding to that story. By watching the faces of these women, by studying their expressions and feelings, by listening to the soundtrack, we each create in our minds vivid versions of the images they seem to be looking at. I guide the audience while it watches *Shirin*, but fully expect and hope that each viewer will, soon enough, let his mind float away and his feelings overflow. Dwell on your own problems and concerns, your own loves and hopes. Let the images flashing through your mind – images aroused by what you see and here – reflect such things.

Shirin is the only one of my films I can watch over and over. Anytime someone wants to see it, I sit with them. It's always different, always a discovery for me. The film came from my realisation that on the rare occasions I went to see a film, I was more interested in the responses of the people sitting next to me than in the action taking place on the screen. I remember feeling envious of a friend because he was able to involve himself in the film, as he watched it, in ways I never could. The roots of *Shirin* probably go back even further. When I was working at the Institute for the Intellectual Development of Children and Young Adults, many decades ago, I designed a poster of an actor peeking through stage curtains, observing the audience before the start of the show. I called it "Wrapped in Viewing the Viewers." I also think about my interest in football, which goes no further than observing the fans. When a match is on television, I would rather have my back to the screen and face the people in the room who are watching, so I can study their reactions. There is something about football that excites even the most serious-minded people. They seem to have an extraordinary capacity for leaving daily concerns behind and abandoning themselves to the game.

When you watch *Shirin*, it looks as though I went to a performance of a Tazieh – a form of theatre – or perhaps even staged one myself, and filmed the close-up responses of more than one hundred women. But it was all shot in the basement of my house in Tehran, and none of the women are actually watching anything. There wasn't much more direction from me than telling each professional actress that she had a few minutes to look at the piece of white paper on the tripod in front of her, onto which I had sketched three stick figures. I asked everyone to act as if she were watching a big screen, responding and moving her eyes from one figure to the next. I used a reflector to create lighting effects on their faces, as if cast from the flicker of light on a screen. When a scene in the film is set indoors there is less light, when the action takes place outside there is more. I asked every actress to recall a personal episode – an intimate memory or emotion – and imagine a film in her mind based on that experience. I suggested that drawing from her own life, not a fictional story, would be the quickest and most effective way of drawing out genuine feeling.

Everything was improvised. Thirty seconds before the actress sat down in the chair, she knew nothing. Sometimes I would ask someone to move in her seat or wipe her eyes or adjust her hijab, and occasionally suggested she was watching something amusing. Every once in a while, when I was sitting at the back of the room, I dropped a metal tray onto the ground as a way of startling the actress. I never told any of them to be sad or gloomy and certainly didn't ask them to cry, though the agreement was that everyone would finish on a sad note. I filmed each woman for five minutes, so ended up with several hundred minutes of footage. Two minutes after being seated, I turned the camera on, and five minutes later it was over. There were several instances when the women had stood up and removed themselves from the camera lens, yet were still deeply involved. The five-minute shoot had ended but the tears hadn't. I found it extraordinary how the vivid imaginations of these women had created and summoned to consciousness such powerful and consequential imagery. The profound emotional upwelling that was provoked became extremely moving to witness.

Afterwards, while editing all those faces together, I added the audio recording of a performance of *Khosrow and Shirin*, a work of ancient Persian literature. I originally hoped to use something else – the soundtrack from Zeffirelli's film version of *Romeo and Juliet* – but couldn't afford the rights. I went through the hours of footage I had captured, picking only those moments I thought were appropriate, then matched the shots with the audio. If the reaction of an actress was compatible with what was happening in the story, I used it. For each scene, I moved the shots around endlessly, until I arrived at the final version. There is an almost unlimited number of ways you could piece together those hundreds of minutes to arrive at a new film. Editing took more than five months. At a certain point, I forced myself to stop.

The film is full of mystery, a conversation with more than one hundred silent women. Study their gazes and see that they are like those of infants in the cradle. Fill each with whatever feelings, emotion and thoughts you want. Will I ever have another chance to stare with such intimacy into so many eyes? The soundtrack somehow turns *Shirin* into an epic love story, but if there is anything of substance in the film, it comes from the audience, from its response to these women. *Shirin* is simultaneously the most artificial and unrealistic film I have ever made, but also one of the most honest and truthful. All I did was pick moments from the footage that somehow reflected the soundtrack. There was only one woman whose performance didn't relate to any part of the story, and it turns out that all she was thinking about during those five minutes was how her dimple would look on camera. I also filmed a couple of non-professional actresses, friends of mine interested in the project, one of whom managed a tear, though later she told me the lights had hurt her eyes.

When you watch *Shirin* you are free to imagine whatever you want, but at the same time – because you are listening to *Khosrow and Shirin* or reading the subtitles, and watching the faces of these women – it could be that you are feeling precisely what I want you to at any moment. Audiences have their freedom, but at the same time are confined within precise boundaries.

❀ ❀ ❀

Art requires appreciation of the enigmatic. It kickstarts the imagination in both creator and audience, leaving behind the rational.

Any response is good. I would rather an audience feel antagonistic towards my work than indifferent. We seek engagement, of any kind.

❂ ❂ ❂

Make your own mind up about everything. A small tree moves out of the shadow of a larger one, in search of sunlight, like a child that wants to grow and blossom by freeing itself from the influence of its parents.

❂ ❂ ❂

What is the least amount of information you can give an audience and still ensure that they know what is happening in your film? What can be omitted? What can you remove and still guide your viewers smoothly from beginning to end?

❂ ❂ ❂

The power of cinema lies in its ability to create believable illusions.

❀ ❀ ❀

Few things I have done professionally started from a deep-rooted or clear intention. Nothing throughout my life ever felt like a planned career. I wandered into the world of cinema by accident and people started calling me a filmmaker. I took many photographs before putting them into an album. Only years later did I show it to people, who then called me a photographer. In Japan, a few years ago, I was asked to sign a visitor's book. I scribbled down a short poem and had fun persuading my hosts that it was by Bashō. When I told them it was actually me who had written it, they suggested I publish my poems, so I collected together some fragments. Now they call me a poet.

I once spoke at a film festival in Isfahan alongside a writer and a book illustrator. The children stared at us with vague looks, and one asked how to become famous. The other speakers talked of perseverance and the difficult paths they had followed since childhood, about how they struggled and invested time in learning their craft. I observed the children's faces as they listened to these success stories, their mouths agape. "Children," I said, when it came to my turn, "without wanting to contradict anyone, my experiences are different. For me it wasn't a struggle. I never had any plans to become a filmmaker. Maybe it's better to put trust in luck and fate than exhaust yourself hoping your life will move in a certain direction. Work hard, of course. Work very hard. But only on whatever you find interesting and joyous. Do that and things you could never have imagined will fall across the path you are walking."

❀ ❀ ❀

Some people set themselves goals in life, but for me it doesn't work like that. Time spent working – painting, making films, writing poetry, taking photographs, doing carpentry, anything at all – is often a response to a profound sense of inadequacy. Anxiety and fear of falling short, dealing with oppressive crises of confidence, are what drive me to do many things. This is somehow a precondition for self-expression. When it comes to creativity, improvement comes from a sense of failure. Disheartened and feeling pathetic, I insist to myself that I am not good enough, that I am not working hard enough. A desire to always do better is what guides.

❂ ❂ ❂

I have always found something foreboding about the wind. I feel agitated by it. My worries reveal themselves in the rush of air. The soul is stirred. I stop whatever I am doing and move towards the window, with interest and fear. Nature takes over the order of things. Nothing is as important as bearing witness to the grandeur and nobility of nature. It's the abandonment of self.

❂ ❂ ❂

If I could spend every hour of the day with the numinous, I would.

❂ ❂ ❂

Popular culture rarely edifies. It pollutes and enervates. I feel truly stunted, even wounded, by it all. Rarely do I watch films these days, and no television, perhaps because it's too passive an act. I always need to be charged up, even though that sometimes means sitting quietly at home. The surge in someone's head can go completely unnoticed, but that doesn't mean it isn't there.

❂ ❂ ❂

Perhaps, the older I get, the less I see. But these days I choose to see less. I choose to notice only what I want to notice. And what I do see is so much brighter than it ever was when I was young.

❂ ❂ ❂

We steadily come to understand what we enjoy doing and what we are good at. Then, hopefully, we spend our lives with those things. Turn your back on everything else. There is little enough time for what we consider worthy of our attention. Let me act like the old man I am. The spirit, the mindset, the approach to life and work that you carry as a youngster is unlikely to change radically as you age. Which is to say: it's never too early to think about such things. Don't waste a single second. Be yourself now.

✿✿✿

It has been many years, but the images and sounds of the home where I grew up – the view from the windows, the creak of the floors, the tiles on the roof, those different silences in each room, the crumbling brickwork – often come to mind.

✿✿✿

Filmmaking isn't the most important thing in my life. These days I feel ambivalent about it. Whenever I am drawn to a film project, I also feel a foreboding, a sense of heaviness. When pre-production takes longer than it should – and it usually does – I tend to get bored. Deep down, I wish something would happen to cause the whole thing to fall apart. The more excited I am about a project, the more I want it to go away. The truth is that I experience a certain relief – even pleasure – when projects I have been working on are cancelled at the last minute. It doesn't bother me if a film of mine is never made. I prefer the films I haven't made to those I have. Even after all these years, whenever there is a substantial break between films, I feel out of practice and am apprehensive about jumping back in.

If I were younger, no doubt my work would be the defining factor of my day-to-day existence, and I would respond to the world in a different way than I do now. As I get older, it becomes ever clearer how I want to live. Being able to eliminate certain things from my life and films – and concentrating on others – has been a slow process for me, a gradual evolution. As I move around the world, from one filming location to another, one festival to the next, I think about going home, closing the door behind me, and leaving everything outside. The "public" Kiarostami doesn't come in with me. Some people are energised in the spotlight, but I am not one of them. I know it doesn't appear to be so, since you can find interviews with me everywhere, but I run from centre stage. I no longer need to be a participant.

✿✿✿

One's inward disposition is louder and stronger than anything that can be imposed upon it. You might be on the right track if what is going on inside your head is of more interest to you than any of the obscurities and distractions offered by the outside world.

I wondered, as a child, if life is about making progress, about achievement and getting on in the world, about creating things that would last as long as anything might last. Or whether life is more about enjoying oneself. I still wonder.

In moments of quiet desperation, feeling disconsolate, I remove myself from the wild currents of ambition by reaching for a book of poetry, and am instantly reminded of the inexhaustible riches that surround us, that a lifetime spent immersed in such a world is a life dignified. And I feel relieved.

✣✣✣

Some of you have asked if you can stay in touch with me. Of course. I welcome it, and will give anyone who asks my email address, which I use occasionally, though I can't promise you will hear back from me promptly. The more forms of connectivity there are, the more I take shelter from such things.

✣✣✣

Life for me has a slow and steady rhythm and pace, something probably reflected in my work. I try to express my ideas in the fewest possible words. I have set myself the goal of finding my place, withdrawing, isolating myself from the chaos, trying to achieve my desire for nothing, for the void. I look upon every film as my last.

✣✣✣

Many young filmmakers want to reinvent the wheel. Most fail, but credit must nonetheless be given to them. Who wants to share space with the unambitious?

✣✣✣

A friend of mine once told me that in person I am, fortunately, not as boring as my films.

165

When I was young, I gave adults my stories to read. They would say, cautiously, that my writing was good, but added, "It's all so pessimistic. Things aren't as bad as all that." It was clear to me these people had given up and sold out to the powers that be, refusing to recognise the bitter, obvious realities of society, oblivious to the despair that creeps up on us all. But today, when young people give me scripts to read, I say, cautiously, "Ingmar Bergman searches in the darkness for a point of light, and it's that point of light which makes his work credible and bearable. You should try it yourself." From the way they look at me, it's evident what they think. I am, for them, past my time. But as I hopefully might have done when I was younger, perhaps they should consider what stage of life I am in. I remember thinking, when making *Taste of Cherry*, that if I could just overcome the hurdles and get past my fifties – the period in life when one's youth is definitively lost and there is a creeping awareness of death – then life would pick up again. And I was right. An Iranian proverb tells us that death is for the person next door.

The older we get, the more able are we to look through other people's eyes. The fact is that my beliefs are born of a lifetime of experience. Even pessimists can't live without hope, which is always worth striving for. In spite of certain difficulties, for several years now, my spirit has been raised, which I think is somehow reflected in my work.

I have spent hours this past week working with you young men and women. Question upon question have been asked of me during these days, and I have dutifully responded. But I couldn't say for sure if any of my utterances have been of use to anyone. I have always felt more comfortable in the realm of images than words, and if I could have just sat, at the back of the room, in silence, showing you a series of pictures, some created by me, some by others, some bright and breezy, some dark and gloomy, some overpowering, some quite everyday, instead of talking, about cinema or anything else, I would have done just that.

A public screening of films made by workshop participants. Standing room only.

I owe you an apology. I confess that when I first looked at this group of you thirty, I thought I was bearing witness to laziness. I should know by now that while the first few days of any workshop are usually a little too slow – even lethargic – for my liking, by the end everything comes together in the most inventive ways. At the start of a workshop, I tend to compare the first days with the final moments of the previous one, when I get to sit and watch all the fine films that have been made. The fact is that it has been beguiling to see the more roisterous of you so drunk with joy at the films you have succeeded in making this week, so free of self-restraint, your minds ablaze and galloping away in new directions. Clearly the toil and sleeplessness was worth the effort, and I applaud your inventiveness. You should all be praised for demonstrating that a single theme can generate an almost unlimited number of ideas. This is the most significant conclusion I have drawn from this week. The other thing to say is that I had a toothache, which coloured my feelings about the work you were doing. Sorry about that.

The community here must disband, but over the coming months I would like to see more films developed from the ideas we have worked on together. Life is one long lesson, which makes this particular week just one small part of an exciting learning curve that you should be forever climbing. I hope you will reflect on your time together here and somehow harness the energy that has been generated over the past few days. In fact, it's your duty to do so. After all, courage and ambition are the lifeblood of art, so acknowledge that the essence of your work should be risk. Never allow that particular fire to be extinguished. Keep it burning within at all times and do not allow anyone to tell you what to do.

Earlier this week I spoke about the childlike qualities of filmmaking, about how the spirit we have as children is steadily scraped away the older we get. We actually come to know less, not more, as we age. Our desires become carefully moderated and worrying about the future turns into a primary preoccupation. So hold onto your youth for as long as possible. Be brash. Cinema survives only because of its constant renewal. Your responsibility as filmmakers is to work hard and experiment, to explore in new directions. Move beyond your customary way of doing things. Break the norms. Look at the world anew each day. Clean out your eyes. Your job is to offer insights, so continue to frame everyday things in new ways that help you, and us, see them differently. The future awaits. As for the filmmaking landscape, each new arrival struggles with the same problems and delights in the same joys. So band together and share everything. There is no one in the world who doesn't have a story to tell.

I ask for your permission to show this collection of short films at other workshops. But before that, we will watch your efforts together here this evening. Some might be better than others, but that's just a matter of taste. What's important is that everyone worked with enthusiasm. I ask that you people sitting in the audience lower your expectations of the films you are going to see. This is the best way to appreciate them. See them with your heart first, and only secondly with your head. We are in a room where you would normally pay good money to be entertained by professionals for two hours. What's important to appreciate is that some of the films about to be screened were made in just a few hours. Each beats with its own heart. Let's have a look.

Published by Sticking Place Books

Lessons with Kiarostami
Edited by Paul Cronin

A Wolf on Watch (dual-language)
Poems by Abbas Kiarostami

With the Wind (dual-language)
Poems by Abbas Kiarostami

Wind and Leaf (dual-language)
Poems by Abbas Kiarostami

Wine (dual-language)
Poetry by Hafez
Selected and adapted by Abbas Kiarostami

Tears (two volumes) (dual-language)
Poetry by Saadi
Selected and adapted by Abbas Kiarostami

Water (dual-language)
Poetry by Nima
Selected and adapted by Abbas Kiarostami

Fire (four volumes) (dual-language)
Poetry by Rumi
Selected and adapted by Abbas Kiarostami

Night (two volumes) (dual-language)
Poetry from the Classical Persian Canon
Selected and adapted by Abbas Kiarostami

Night (two volumes) (dual-language)
Poetry from the Contemporary Persian Canon
Selected and adapted by Abbas Kiarostami

In the Shadow of Trees
The Collected Poetry of Abbas Kiarostami